S0-BSX-089

The
Living Testify

Copyright © Gefen Publishing House Ltd.
Jerusalem 1994/5754

All rights reserved. No part of this publication may be translated, reproduced,
stored in a retrieval system or transmitted, in any means, electronic,
mechanical, photocopying, recording or otherwise, without express written
permission from the publishers.

Typeset: Marzel Translation, Jerusalem

Cover Design: Helen Twena/Gefen

ISBN 965-229-105-6

Edition 9 8 7 6 5 4 3 2 1

Gefen Publishing House Ltd.   Gefen Books
P.O.B. 6056, Jerusalem   12 New St., Hewlett
91060 Israel   N.Y., U.S.A. 11557

Printed in Israel

The Living Testify

Edited by Moshe Davis and Meir Hovav
Adapted from the Hebrew by Moshe Kohn

For Beit HaEdut – Testimony House for
the Zionist Heritage and Remembrance of the Shoah

gefen publishing house בית הוצאה לאור גפן

In memory of
those who are ever with us

On this fiftieth year
commemorating the Hungarian Shoah and
Redemption of the Spared Remnant

Nir Galim   Beit HaEdut
1994   5754

Table of Contents

Moshe Davis

'I have two grandpas, two grandmas'

For a little while I forsook you, but with vast love I will bring you back.

Isaiah 54:7

I have been granted the *zechut*, the privilege, of serving dear friends – Holocaust orphans, builders of Nir Galim, an agricultural settlement on the outskirts of Ashdod, and bringing their innermost thoughts to the attention of the world. Why? The reason is beyond me, but this is how it came about.

My wife Lottie, our young children, Zev and Tamar, and I came as guests for Rosh Hashanah 5711-1950 to the settlement of Nir Galim. We formed close ties with the community, and later, when we came to settle in Israel, were accepted as honorary members of the moshav. Although from different continents and cultures, through spiritual affinity we became one. Common ancestral custom – the traditions of Eastern European Jewry – joined us together. As the bonds of friendship deepened, Lottie and I felt free to inquire into their lives. Their stories became clear only through respectful listening, embracing their lives in their parental homes, their odysseys from suffering to redemption, their powerful desire to build and be rebuilt in Zion's Land.

In the spring of 1954 I was invited to deliver the American Jewish Tercentenary lectures at the Hebrew University of Jerusalem and elsewhere in Eretz Yisrael, commemorating the first settlement of Jews in New Amsterdam in 1654. It was then, during Shabbat prayers at Nir Galim, that the seeds of the testimonies contained in this volume were planted in the furrows of my being.

Services were held in the enlarged wooden hut that was combination dining hall, assembly room, and social center. We sat on rickety benches, with our prayer books and Torah commentaries duly aligned on a shaky table covered with white cloth. Beside me sat a *haver*, fervent in prayer. At a pause in the service, aware that I shared the pent-up pain of those victims of the Destruction, and knowing that my vocation was the study of contemporary Jewry, he exclaimed – I vividly recall that first outpouring of self, in a whispered cry: "How can I explain to the children that I and my wife aren't Adam and Eve?"

3

I was dumb. He did not expect an answer. The reading of the Torah continued. We parted, but the seed began to germinate.

My family came on *aliyah* in 1959. Nir Galim became our second home. Then came the beginning of the response to my neighbor's question, in shattering and agonizing form, as we stood once again together at prayer.

The core group of Nir Galim survivors had come from Hungary. Stark figures and dates record that the German occupation of Hungary began March 19, 1944, though the beginning of the end of Hungarian Jewry actually started a few days earlier. On May 15, the first deportation left, and in the ensuing weeks 437,402 Jews were ruthlessly cast out of the five zones organized by the Germans. Ninety-five percent of the deportees were entrained in boxcars to Auschwitz, imprisoned in barracks, and hastily prepared for the mass murder. By the time the Russians overran Hungary in January 1945, of the approximately 825,000 Hungarian Jews in 1941, 565,000 had perished, and 260,000 survived the Shoah, among them the forty-six witnesses in this volume.

The families of most Nir Galim survivors had lived in eastern and north-eastern Hungary. Their deportations had taken place mainly after Pesach, in April 1944, and continued for three months through the 17th day of Tammuz, the date that in the Jewish calendar marks the launching of the sieges of Jerusalem that ended in the destructions of the First and Second Temples.

During those weeks, I was startled to see the rare scenes of multiple *aliyot* to the Torah, with many in the congregation rising to recite Kaddish. Question turned to pain when I learned that these survivors, who did not know the dates of their bereavements, had been bidden by the rabbis of Hungary to observe the annual memorial on the day their loved ones had been expelled to Auschwitz. Why did they not observe the mourning period in Hungary itself upon their return? Because hope was never forlorn. Perhaps...

The Adam and Eve expression continued to gnaw at me. I read and heard various explanations, and in the end heard another one, an answer unique to a group of people like the survivors at Nir Galim. This was: the need to bring out all that they were carrying within them, to speak out the full truth, only gradually, if need be, in stammers and stutters wherever that would be the case, so that their children and grandchildren and all their posterity would know.

The members of Nir Galim rarely spoke of themselves. Most of their "small talk" whenever they happened to meet, or at their scheduled get-togethers, centered on current events and the problems facing the Jewish People and Israel. From time to time, a desire to delve more methodically into these questions was expressed, and it was suggested that I lead

4

a group that would study Diaspora Jewry, along the lines of the study circle I was then conducting in Jerusalem under the auspices of the President of Israel.

The Nir Galim study group was initiated in 1983; each year we chose to explore a different topic. A nucleus of regular participants emerged; the overwhelming majority of them included the moshav's founders, that is, the Holocaust survivors.

In 1987, I sensed that the time was ripe to face the challenge directly. I suggested to the group that the topic of that year's study should be themselves, that together we should try to probe their own histories, their imprisonment and release, and *aliyah* to Eretz Israel. The object would be the subject! Can there be a more primary source?

As an academic, I was, of course, familiar with the "oral history" method of gathering group testimony. I was well aware of the extent to which the solidity and value of the testimony depends on the ability of the witness to overcome inhibitions and fears. Here I was helped by the head and staff of the Yad Vashem Martyrs' and Heroes' Remembrance Authority. Through Dr. Shmuel Krakowsky, then director of the Yad Vashem archive, I invited members of the Nir Galim group to Jerusalem. There, at Yad Vashem, I explained what I hoped to do. At first, the response was utter silence. I explained again, mentioning the synchronized efforts to deny that the Holocaust ever occurred, and I declared that it was our responsibilty to the generations to speak out. Silence. I waited. At last, one of the women, who had never said a word to her children about her experiences as a girl in the Holocaust, said, "I'll speak."

Forty-six separate, individual testimonies were recorded, supervised by Adina Ben-Shemesh, assisted by Dr. Leon Volovici and Dr. Gavriel Bar-Shaked. An archive was set up at Nir Galim to preserve this documentation, and the witnesses each received a copy of their testimony.

We wondered what further could be done with the accumulated material. The study group's coordinating committee met at the home of my friend, the writer Aharon Appelfeld, in joint consultation with Professor Netanel Katzburg and writer-editor Yoel Rappel. After much discussion, we decided to continue the effort to elicit fuller testimonies at Nir Galim, and to publish a volume of extracts from the testimonies already gathered.

Published in Hebrew in 1990 as *Eda'i Hayim*, co-edited with Meir Hovav, was the first message of remembrance. This edition of the book for Israeli readers has had three printings, and another is in press. With the establishment of Beit Ha Edut – Testimony Center of Religious Zionism and the Holocaust – at Nir Galim, under the visionary chairmanship of Shraga Shemer, and with the steady stream of visitors from abroad, we were urged to prepare an English adaptation of the volume. Eventually, the complete testimony archive will be published, God willing, until all has been told and heard.

In reciting the story of the book's unfolding in detail, I wish to show that those like myself, who grew up far from the scenes of the destruction of European Jewry, can also have a role in learning and transmitting the truth of the events of those years. In joining those who suffered so immeasurably, we can also perpetuate the remembrance of those whose names are recorded in the "scroll of fire."

Remembrance alone, however, is not all. The living witnesses of Nir Galim have demonstrated how it is possible to rebuild one's personal and group life through a common aspiration to create a future together. In this volume we honor their strength, not only in bitter adversity, but in rebuilding, and having the courage to share their life stories with us and future generations.

Erev Yom Hazikaron, Remembrance Day
Rosh Hashanah, 5754 (1993-4)
Moshe, child of Avigdor Halevi and Idie Davis

F.S. (Futurescript) Several weeks ago, after ushering in the month of Elul, with all the tones of the coming High Holy Days, my neighbor suggested that we walk to our homes together. He was excited, and walked with a spring in his gait, joy reflected in his eyes. He grasped my arm. "I never dreamed this would happen," he almost shouted, "Imagine! My grandson, impetuously grasped my foot the other day and blurted out of the blue: I have *two* grandpas, *two* grandmas. Our son, born during our internment in Cyprus in 1948, thought we were Adam and Eve."

My neighbor's name is Nehemia – "God comforts."

PROCLAMATION

In the Name of the Rabbis of Hungary
With God's Help

To Our Godfearing Jewish Brethren in Our Land, and Their Rabbis andf Communal Leaders

In order to commemorate the great catastrophe that befell the Jewish People with the murder and burning of thousands – myriads – of our brethren from the year 5701 (1941) on, especially in the years 5704 and 5705, and with the destruction of the synagogues and study-houses, and the loss of Torah Scrolls and other sacred writings that are the stock of every Jewish home, it behooves us to proclaim a communal fast day.

We have chosen the 20th day of the month of Sivan, because most of the murders were perpetrated in this month, and because this date was already established as a communal fast day in Poland.

This day is therefore declared a day to be observed throughout the land...

It is proper on this day to preach to the public, speaking words of chastisement – words spoken from the heart that will enter the hearts of all our brethren and move them to full repentance.

Let every effort be made to see to it that the entire public participates – men, women and children – so that all may be moved to mend their ways. As a result, perhaps the Creator will show mercy to His wretched people, and He Who told His universe "No more" will also say "No more" to our travails, that we may see the world redeemed.

May the Guardian of Israel safeguard the remnants of His People Israel by gathering all the scattered of Israel and sending the True Redeemer soon in our time, so that this day and all fast days shall be transformed into days of rejoicing and festivity.

The Central Bureau of the Congregation of the Pious
Pest, the month of Iyar 5706 (1946)

Joshua Yehoshua Amsel

Born 1922 in Nyirbeltek, Hungary. There and in Budapest till April 1943. Forced-labor unit at Zombor, spring 1943. Bor, Yugoslavia, July. Changes in Hungarian command and worsening treatment of Jews, April 1944. March from Bor to Belgrade and massacre at Cservenka, September 1944. Labor camps at Mohacs and Szentkiraly Szabadia. Camps in Germany – Uhrdorf and Bergen-Belsen – till liberation. Zionist training camp in Hungary till move to Israel, 1948.

What life was like there

On November 25 we travelled to Uhrdorf. At that stage I already realized what was going on in the camps. I had been right in the Valley of Slaughter and still I had not believed that human beings were capable of such things. There was one positive thing about me: I didn't want to die. I may have that to thank for my survival. Already in November I saw the Allied airplanes. I reckoned that the war would soon be over. I told myself: "Yehoshua, we're going to try our hardest. You don't have to die." But how do you do this?

At Uhrdorf, the Nazi command staff was helped to run things by prisoners assigned to various jobs – as *Blockaelteste* (block chiefs) and *Zimmeraelteste* (room chiefs), and also as kitchen staff. Ukrainians and Russians worked in the kitchens. The Russians were comparatively decent. The Ukrainians were terrible. I think that group included some Jews. I knew of one Jew, a Communist, and several times I wanted to go over to him and ask for a job in the kitchen, but I was afraid I might be made a *kapo*, and people in that post were in the habit of hitting and harassing people, and sometimes even killing.

Every morning we walked from camp to the nearby town. From there we rode about 20-30 kilometers. We were laying a rail line. When we set out for work, we would be given a loaf of bread for every five men, and on our return in the evening we got two bowls of soup. The work was overseen by SS men who patrolled the area. There were two problems: hunger and cold. The cold was the more serious problem. We had cloth hats, like those bakers wear, one pair of pants, a battle jacket and a belt to protect the kidneys – a flannel strip, to keep the cold out. That was all we wore.

One day a Jew from Munkacs, who felt very cold, came over alongside me. We were working with pickaxes and the ground was frozen. He didn't work, and actually I didn't either. But as soon as I saw the SS man approaching, I would lift my pickaxe and let it fall. One day the SS man noticed that the Jew beside me wasn't doing any work, and he ordered me in German to show the man what to do. I explained to that Munkacs Jew in Hungarian how to do the job: "You lift the pickaxe and bring it down, lift and down," and I added, in Hungarian, "*tovább is*," meaning, "and so on." At this the SS man drew his pistol from his holster and cocked it. "Why, *Kamerad*?" I asked as calmly as I could. "You're a Communist," he replied. "You said '*tovarisch*'" [the Russian Communist salutation meaning 'comrade']. I explained that what I had said was "*tovább is*," Hungarian for "and so on," and that he could confirm this by asking anyone who spoke Hungarian. He returned the pistol to the holster. From this you can tell what little value life had there: nothing, zero. Such things happened. What could a person do at such moments, run away? There was nowhere to run. It's a good thing I was capable of asking "Why?" If I had tried to run, he'd have killed me.

Wife:	Naomi			
Children:	Tzvi	Uri	Rivka	Moshe
Grand-children:	Orit	Tamar		
	David	Nir		
	Naama	Erez		
	Einat			

Naomi Amsel (nee Ehrenfeld)

Born 1926 at Hajduszoboszlo, Hungary. To Puspokladany. Father drafted into Hungarian Army, then, in 1943, into army labor unit. Twenty-two Jewish heads of families murdered in Puspokladany, 1944. Germans enter town, Jews concentrated in local ghetto in May. Debrecen ghetto. To Auschwitz, June. Life in Birkenau camp. To Ravensbrueck camp, August 15. To Altenburg, August 23. Life in camp till April 1945. From Ravensbruck to Waldenburg. Liberation, April 1945. Rehabilitation. To Eretz Yisrael on s. s. Kedma, 1948.

Sensitive children

Before being deported to Auschwitz, we had been concentrated in the Debrecen area. The place we were in had been a leather factory. Living conditions were indescribable. The latrines were open holes and many people fell into them. My mother's mother was with us. At home she had already had problems connected with old age, and her memory failed her. The poor woman didn't know where she was and she wanted to go home, saying: "I don't want to go into these toilets – you can fall into the holes. I don't want to eat – it isn't clean here."

One day the Germans announced they were taking families with four children and men with trades to Debrecen. My brother decided that we would go. After we had said goodbye to Grandma and to our aunts, my mother started crying: How could she leave them all? But my brother insisted. Mama said: "But you're not a carpenter!" My brother replied: "I'll know how to do what they want." And we went.

We took along some linens and a thin feather quilt to cover ourselves with at night. It was a march of eight or nine kilometers. We were weak and our morale was very low. We didn't know where we were going or why. My mother was in very bad condition. She cried all the way, sobbing that she would never see her mother again. But my brother suddenly turned man, and his conduct was extraordinary. He was a scholar, and everybody knew him. I was the disorganized one. I was 18 then and my brother was 15.

We arrived at the Debrecen ghetto and all of a sudden we were among total strangers. Mama was frightened and didn't want to stay. The place looked outlandish to us.

Two hours later the Germans showed up. They didn't encourage the people to join the family groups or the skilled workers, and they took advantage of the confusion. They announced that anyone wishing to go back to the places they had come from could do so. Mama begged my brother to go back: "We don't have anyone here. We don't know a soul. What if Papa gets a furlough? Where will he look for us? Maybe he'll be able to take us to the place where he's working, and you'll also be able to work there, as a carpenter!"

She pleaded and begged so much, I think that I and my brother couldn't take it any more. We were sensitive children, and we said: "All right, let's go back."

As soon as we set out it began to rain – a hot, heavy summer rain. Do you have any idea how much rain a feather quilt can absorb? And how heavy the quilt becomes as a result? The three of us began to tote the quilt, but it got so heavy that in the end we just threw it away. We noticed that many people before us had thrown things away. Now we were left without anything.

We were back. Grandma didn't recognize us. Things were so bad that her condition deteriorated rapidly till she didn't know where she was any more.

It was evening when we got back. We had nothing to cover ourselves with and nothing to eat. Now we didn't have a thing, and people collected things for us. One family gave us a blanket and that night we slept curled up with my mother under that blanket.

We were in that camp a week. On Sunday afternoon we were taken to Auschwitz.

Husband: Yehoshua

Offspring: Listed with testimony of husband, Yehoshua Amsel

Nehemiah David

Born 1924 in Nagyida, Transylvania. Life in Nagyida village. Forsakes idea of escaping to Rumania. Szaszragen ghetto. How Jews saw Hungarians and Rumanians. Drafted for forced labor. In Nagybanya camp. Easier work in Budapest area thanks to prior acquaintance with Hungarian officer. Dispatch of labor unit to Austrian border and escape to Budapest. Released, re-drafted into labor unit. Trial at Szombathely. Labor camp in Austria. Religious observance in camp. German retreat and liberation by Russians. Year in Nagyida. Attitude of local populace. Conversation with village's two priests. Displaced-persons' camps in Austria. To Israel in 1949 from British internment camp in Cyprus.

My honor

On my journey home to the village, I wondered what it would be like. I surveyed the area from the ridge. From that height, you could see a great distance. I saw our vineyard, the fields, our houses. I recalled the dreams I had dreamt about being a tree – part of that countryside, part of those mountains, belonging to them. I thought about what had been done to the Jewish People in general and to my family in particular. About how all that was beautiful in Man – here likened to the beautiful natural landscape, the mountains – had descended to such depths, to such unprecedented cruelty. How wretched for humanity! Towards what end?! How is it said? – "What is my crime, what is my sin?" Nature is so gorgeous. I remembered the Sabbaths, the festivals, among our extended family. We would go into the countryside: the stillness, the pure air, the beauty, the harmony – there was room for all. You didn't see anyone push. There was no wickedness there. Everybody and everything was forbearing, patient, as though some Hand were directing everything thus. Everything was alive, everything grew, with nothing and no one interfering. It hurts so – what human being are capable of doing to each other.

Why, I mused, go into the village by daylight, to see the man you lived with, grew up with, went to school with, trusted, helped in good times and bad, shared his joys? I didn't want them running after me saying: "Here he is, poor fellow..."

I couldn't forget those moments when they didn't stand by our side - not a single one of them – not the Rumanians, not the Hungarians, not the Saxonians. I didn't want to see them at the moment of my homecoming.

I walked on. It was turning dark. It was May, springtime. The young people were outside. I recognized many of them, to the right and to the left. I didn't answer them. They called out: "There's a stranger in the village!" One of them followed

me and recognized me. He let out a shout: "Nehemiah!" It turned into a circus.
All of a sudden they were all friends: "Come over to our house! You'll have a
meal with us! How we cried for you, how it hurt us to see how they humiliated
you!" I said: "No! I want to go see my honor." "What honor?" "Our house! I want
to see what kind of respect you paid our house. I want to see what condition
it's in." Not a soul was there. I went into the rooms – no door, no window, no
table, not a single piece of furniture... The house was empty. The winepress was
empty. Books – volumes of the Mishna and Talmud, festival prayerbooks – piled
up in the yard, soaked from rain and snow. Pictures – one or two.

It was evening and the older people came, Hungarians: "Young man, come over
to us, come and sit with us; why stay here alone?" I said: "No, thanks." There was
no one in the village who didn't come and shake his head.

The next day I went to the vineyard. Here a big surprise awaited me: in the
middle of the vineyard there came running toward me – Who? - My only true
friend, who really didn't know how to lie, and I believed him – I mean the dog.
He gave me a proper welcome. A human-on-four. He didn't budge from me,
didn't forsake me for a moment. The cat also came back. Afterwards all the
members of my family arrived. We were four brothers and sisters. We
rehabilitated everything – the vineyard, the trees. But to enjoy life there?!... Not
for a single moment did I consider staying. Every minute, every second I thought
of nothing but going to live in Eretz Yisrael. I spent nearly a year in the village. I
had returned in May 1945 and I left the place in March 1946.

Wife:	Rahel	
Children:	Dani	Menahem
Grand-children:	Hanan	Rivka
	Yaron	Ze'ev
	Yonatan	Moshe
	Avishai	Gila
	Oriel	
	Eilon	

Hanna Deutsch (nee Frenkel)

Born 1930 in Vasarosnameny, Hungary. Parents' home. Schoolday memories. Expulsion of families lacking Hungarian citizenship. Collecting money to bribe authorities in Budapest. Family's economic situation after father declared missing. April 1944: Jews concentrated in Beregszasz ghetto. Deportation to Auschwitz. "Selections" and living conditions in Auschwitz. Hanna and sister deported to Germany. Markleeberg camp. Work in factory making airplane spare parts till evacuation in spring 1945. Work on German peasant's farm before and after liberation. Russian soldiers. Return to Budapest via Prague, and return to Vasarosnameny. Loss of belongings that had been hidden. Year in Vac. At camp for young girls of Bnai Akiva religious Zionist youth movement. Difficulties in getting out of Communist Hungary. Smuggling Jews out of country. Failed attempt to steal across Slovakian border. Arrest. Another effort to leave Hungary, 1949. Arrival in Israel in 1949 after stay in Austria and Italy. Attitude to Holocaust. Attitude to visits in Germany and Hungary.

A 'good' camp

Compared to the other camps, the Markleeberg camp near Leipzig was a good one. It was a small camp for women, mainly from Hungary, and in my estimation there were no more than 4,000 women there; some say even less. We worked in a factory making spare parts for airplanes. We – that is: I, my sister, my cousin and about 20 other girls – were lucky. We only had to do a 12-hour day shift, while the others had to alternate between day and night shifts. Our setup had a big advantage. The others were jealous of us. We were given lunch in the factory consisting of a loaf of bread, margarine and victuals. People didn't grab. Everything was done in orderly fashion. On Sundays we didn't work; we just did our laundry and washed up.

My foreman was a German Socialist and he always brought us the latest news about the war. His secretary was a very fat woman. She wore a swastika on her chest, and she had a son serving in the SS, yet she was very good to me. Every morning, when I rinsed her coffee cup, I knew she had saved a thin slice of bread for me. She gave me an extra undergarment so I should be warm. And the foreman always gave me a smile. The guarding of the camp was done mainly by SS women, and the camp commander was also decent to us. I and my sister took care how we looked: we wanted to look as pretty as possible. We painted the wooden shoes we had been issued in the camp dark-gray.

The foreman saw what we had done but didn't say a word. He seemed to like it. Usually people were tried and punished for such things.

There were all kinds of punishments. The work was checked, and it was forbidden to work without wearing a frock over our clothing. I felt very warm and I took off the frock. I was punished. I had to stand beside the fence for many hours. There was another thing I was afraid of. I was wearing an extra undergarment, the one I had been given by the German woman. That was also something for which they punished people. I was ready to stand there wearing just one garment, but my sister took my frock and stood there instead of me. There was still another punishment, an ugly one. Belgian, Russian and Dutch prisoners-of-war worked in the factory. They were the foremen. They trained the girls, and no conversation was allowed except about the work. Some girls were caught conversing. Our hair had begun to grow. The girls who were caught had a strip shaved up the middle of their skull. It was an awful sight, awful. They stood out so. Afterwards we were told that one of the Belgian young men fell in love with one of the girls. They got married later. Yes, love also flourished there. This camp can't be compared to other camps.

One day we were told that a baby had been born at the hospital. The camp commander offered to be the baby's godfather. We told ourselves that if that was the case, then we were not badly off. But it seems that the authorities had other ideas. We heard that the mother and baby were taken away. We don't know where they were taken.

Husband:	Yeshayahu		
Children:	Shabtai	Eliezer	Rahel
Grand-children:	Vered	Dror	Iddo
	Ayelet	Hagit	Amit
	Aviad	Orit	
	Chen	Azriel	
		Dvir	

15

Yeshayahu Deutsch

Born 1927 in Bodrog-Keresztur, Hungary. Parents' home in Bodrog-Keresztur. Intensification of antisemitism till 1944. Germans enter. Antisemitic reaction of commander of Hungarian youth military formation for failure to wear Star of David patch. Jews concentrated in Satoraljaujhely. Train journey to Auschwitz. Deutsch and brother sent on transport to Warsaw. Clearing ruins and removing bricks from destroyed buildings till August 1944. Death march to Auschwitz. People distributed among different labor camps. Kaufering camp. Evacuation from camp and march to Dachau, April 1945. Encounter with Americans and liberation at Alach six kilometers from Dachau.

No patch, no defense

The Germans entered Bodrogkeresztur after Purim. Immediately anti-Jewish edicts were issued, including one to wear the Star of David patch on the outer garment. I vividly remember the arrival of the Germans because of something that happened to me. It was Friday afternoon. I had been sent to get wine for the Sabbath *Kiddush* rite, at a shop about 50 or 60 meters from our home. On the way back I ran into one of the commanders of the Hungarian youth pre-army formation, the Levente, a sergeant, who was riding his bicycle. He stopped me and said: "Kike! Why aren't you wearing your patch? You're coming with me to Tokay, where I'm handing you over to the Germans! You trot ahead of me!" I started trotting. People who saw me hurried to tell my parents. Afterwards I learned that this commander had a superior who was on good terms with a Tokay Jew and could be bought off. Mama rushed to that Jew in Tokay. Riding there, she passed me trotting ahead of the sergeant on his bicycle, on our way to Tokay six kilometers away. When we arrived, a Jew was waiting for us. He stopped the sergeant and asked him where his commander was. He also asked about me: "What did this kid do to you?" The sergeant answered: "He isn't wearing the patch, and I'm handing him over to the Germans." I was taken to the headquarters in Tokay. Hungarian gendarmes were there. They didn't ask me a thing, just locked me up in the cellar. An hour and a half later the sergeant came down. He looked at my watch and asked how I got it. I said it was a Bar-Mitzva present. He took the watch, saying: "I'm taking the watch. Don't you tell anyone! I'm letting you go. There's a Jew waiting for you outside. You'll be with him for the Sabbath."

Outside, that Jew was waiting for me, and he invited me to spend the Sabbath with him. He promised to speak to the senior officer. It was still light outside and I preferred to run the six kilometers home. I didn't tell him about the watch that had been stolen from me; I was afraid. But at home I told them. At home and in the village they were surprised that that sergeant, who didn't even live in the village, had dared to behave like that. But he knew me from the Levente, he was an antisemite, and he knew about the edict requiring us to wear the patch.

Wife: Hanna

Offspring: Listed with testimony of wife, Hanna Deutsch

Shlomo Donath, *of blessed memory*

Born in Beregszasz, Slovakia. In Beregszasz till 1939. In labor units in labor camps at Satoraljauhely, Kosice, Munkacs and Dolina till German occupation. From Beregszasz ghetto to Auschwitz. Member of Communist underground in Auschwitz. Liberation and stay in Cracow. Return to Beregszasz in February 1945. To Eretz Yisrael in 1948.

'The Russians are coming! The Russians are coming!'

Early in January we heard the shooting. One day they had everybody line up in the yard, gave each person a piece of sausage and bread, and took them all on a march outside the camp. I was in hospital at the time. There were two barracks with beds containing people condemned to death. There were doctors, but they weren't able to do much without drugs and equipment. I lay there with 850 patients: half of them were dead.

Shortly before the evacuation I pleaded with a young doctor, Kraus: "Do me a favor, Dr. Kraus, and take me out of here. If I stay, they'll kill me." He said: "If you go out into that frost with 40 degrees [centigrade] fever, you're sure to be dead inside of a few minutes. Stay here, and if you believe in God or miracles – who knows? – maybe a miracle will happen."

He gave me some sulfa tablets and said: "That's a week's supply. If you take them over two days, maybe it will do some good." That is what I did, and fortunately, within two days my temperature went down.

On the eve of the evacuation Russian airplanes appeared and bombed the industrial zone. One of the bombs – perhaps a flare bomb – fell on the other side of the camp. The wooden barracks and straw mattresses burned like paper. The wind swept the flames along, and the barracks went up in flames one after the other in domino fashion. Forty rows of barracks. We didn't dare go outside, as SS men were still riding by on motor scooters. But it was also dangerous to remain inside, because of the blaze. A miracle happened: just a few rows before the hospital, the wind suddenly changed direction, and the barracks there started burning. We remained with the patients.

Of those who remained, I was one of the strongest. You can imagine how strong I was at 42 kilograms. I was the doctor, having once studied medicine. I did the best I could. I brought some water to drink. I replaced a bandage with a strip of rag. There was no food. But I and a young fellow from Holland found some potatoes. We boiled them in melted snow and gave a potato to every patient who could eat. A few days passed between the departure of the Germans and the Russians' arrival. During this time about half the patients died. I and the Dutchman dragged them outside and piled up the bodies, so there should be room in the barrack. We had no feelings at all for the dead. We had seen so many horrors, so much death, that this no longer shocked us. I told those able to move that they should not go outside. We feared that there were still some Germans in the area.

One day I saw an unidentified group of soldiers going towards the front, in the direction of Cracow. I had no idea who they were or in which language to ask them. In Jewish style I gestured with my hands, as if to ask: "*Nu!?* What's this?" Someone shouted to us: "What? You don't know? The Russians are here! You're free! The Russians are coming!" I went into the barrack and said to those who still had a spark of life in them: "People: we're free! The Russians are coming! The Russians are coming!" Everybody shouted: "Hurrah!" The roof didn't rise, of course, but they said it with all the strength that still remained in them: "Hurrah!"

Wife:	Malka, of blessed memory		
Children:	Tzipora	Tzvi	Ilana	Doron
Grand-children:	David	Hadar	Malka	Orr
	Dan	Yisrael	Eyal	Noam
	Oded	Hanna		
	Shlomo	Shlomo		
		Yael		
		Esther		
		Hodaya		

Yisrael Feld

Born 1928 in Satoraljaujhely, Hungary. Parents can't get Hungarian citizenship; expelled to Ukraine. Flight during murders at Kamenitz-Podolsk. Attempt to reach Hungary; arrested after someone informs. Detention camp in Hungary till 1943. Refugees bring news from Czechoslovakia and Poland. Privileges to communal leaders till deportation to Auschwitz. Transfer to Durnau camp. How different prisoners cope with plight. Flossenburg camp. Death march. Return to Hungary. Zionist training camp. To Israel, 1948.

They won't take it out of your belly

After the air raid along the way, they collected all the people who had been hit. Instead of treating them, someone with scissors simply went around snipping as needed – a hand, a foot. Sheared them off like trouser fabric, and tied them; those who had the strength did their own tying. Some of those hit – whether killed or just wounded – were piled up criss-cross, the way freshly cut logs are piled in the forest. I can still see that sight next to the rail line. They piled them up the way wooden carts are sometimes piled in rows alongside the railroad tracks. Inside the pile there were some people who were still alive. But we paid no attention. Our minds were no longer functioning enough for us to notice. When we had got ourselves reorganized, I started entering the wagons to see if there was anyone from my town, somebody Hungarian. In one wagon I saw someone from Ungvar. "Who is that?" It seems it was the younger of two brothers who had been with us. He was so exhausted that he didn't have the strength to come out of the wagon. I went over to him and asked: "What happened to my brother? What happened to *your* brother?" He answered: "We ran away! I didn't have any strength left, so they put me on the train and they continued walking." That was the last bit of information I got about my brother. Meanwhile, they re-assembled us. They got the wagons ready, brought a locomotive and repaired the rails. Again they packed us into the wagons. We didn't eat a thing, because they didn't give us any food. Only at the beginning of our journey, before we boarded the wagons, they gave everyone a portion or two of bread, which was supposed to suffice for the entire trip. They didn't give us a thing after that. I don't even remember us drinking water. I had already eaten my bread. I had already learned from experience not to save bread for the next day. It was when I was still together with my brother. He had less will power than I when it came to going without food. He always ate up his ration while I left some over. The next afternoon, while I was eating the bread I had saved, he would ask me for some and I gave him. In the evening he would pay me back, and he had less to eat. The next day I would again have some "extra" bread, and again I would give him some. Then I told him: "You know what? Don't pay me back. Let's make a common pantry. We'll combine our rations and we'll save some and eat it together. I'll do the dividing." He was always very hungry, and so was I, but I seem to have had more will power, or my body didn't need as much food. Then – I remember: we had a bigger ration of bread, and I wrapped it well and put it under my head before we went to sleep. The next morning it was gone. My brother cursed me: "Not only didn't we eat it, but we don't have anything left! From now on I'm finishing my bread the second I get it." I also learned the lesson: I ate up my food the moment I got it. What is already inside the belly is there to stay; nobody will take it out of there.

Wife: Yael

Children: Sarah   Nava   Nurit   Anat   Tali   Daniella

Grand-   Hadas Yaarit Shahar Netanel
children: Avital Mor   Liron   Shir
          Re'ut   Yaniv   Avimeir
          Tamar   Sivan   Mattan
                  Maayan

21

Berta Fon (nee Katz)

Born 1928 in Ruscova, Transylvania. Life hard for Jews in Ruscova; worsens with entry of Hungarians in August 1940. German behavior in early stages of occupation. Viso ghetto. Auschwitz. In transport of 2,000 women to Upper Silesia. Building bomb shelters for German Army. With sister in death march from Upper Silesia, January 1945. Liberated in Teresienstadt, May 1945. Sails for Eretz Yisrael with Agudat Yisrael group on s.s. Knesset Yisrael. Battle with British and internment in Cyprus till June 1947, then to Eretz Yisrael.

The death march

We were about 2,000 women in the camp in Upper Silesia. We were there from the end of September 1944 till January 1945. In January we set out on a long, arduous march. It was winter. Our shoes were worn out and our clothes were tattered. We walked about 30 kilometres a day through villages, hamlets, woods. Sometimes, when we made a stop, we got something to drink and a bite of food. Not enough, though. We were forced to find ways to keep ourselves alive. We were escorted by SS soldiers. Those who foraged for sugar beet or other victuals were severely beaten. Many were the nights we went to sleep without eating a thing. We became steadily weaker. At first we dragged along the women who were unable to walk. We made stretchers of a sort out of logs and blankets, and we took turns carrying. The Germans said they would send the weak ones by train, but when we got to places where there was no habitation, they would leave the weak ones there. After we had moved off, we would hear gunshots. We presumed that they killed those women. After a while the Germans stopped trying to hide what they were doing. More than once as we walked, a woman would plump herself down on the ground totally exhausted, and if anyone stopped to try to help her, the Germans would shoot the two women right before our eyes. In the first weeks that was very painful and we cried. But the march lasted quite a few weeks, and we suffered so much and so long that we stopped feeling it after a while.

We passed through towns whose names I no longer remember. The population was German, and the people were well dressed. They did not try to strike up conversations with us, and they seemed to regard us as a passing circus.

We didn't know in which direction we were marching, and I can't remember the names of the towns and camps. I remember arriving at the Ravensbrueck camp. At a certain point we were joined by non-Jewish prisoners – men and women – from other camps. After Ravensbrueck, we were put in open wagons with non-Jewish male prisoners. At first, I and my sister tried to keep ourselves clean. We had a comb. We tried to keep our distance from the crowd. But it was cold in the wagon, and we huddled in order to keep warm. We were crawling with lice. It was possible to see them, and to brush them off with our hands. It was terribly packed in the wagon. To make a little space we piled the corpses along the sides and sat on them. I don't remember that shocking us. After the train trip, we were put in a big barn and kept there a while.

In Auschwitz, my sister had managed – to this day I don't know how – to hide a gold chain. She tore it in two. In exchange for half of the chain, we were able to get food for a while. I was 16; my sister was three and a half years older than me. She always looked for ways to keep us alive. In a stall we once found a sackful of wheat. That sustained us for quite a few days. She suggested that we should always save a piece of bread for harder times. Sometimes we found some sugar beet in the field, or, less frequently, radish. If we reached an inhabited area before dark, she would sometimes, despite the great risk, sneak into one of the farmyards and occasionally succeed in getting some victuals. I remember once getting a potato, and we thought that was a great thing. A potato, even a raw one, was a real delicacy. If not for my sister, I wouldn't have survived that long, arduous route to Teresienstadt.

Husband:	Shimon			
Children:	David,* (of blessed memory)	Dina*	Haya**	Shula**
Grand-children:		Rahel Chen David Ayala Naftali	David Matanya	Tali Yonatan Yael

* children of Rahel, of blessed memory
** daughters of David Katz, of blessed memory

Shimon Fon

Born 1926 in Mezokovesd, Hungary. At Gyongyos till German occupation. In forced-labor units in Eger district. At farm near Gyongyos. Building the Kiskunfeleyhaza airfield 26 kilometers south of Budapest. Escape to Budapest, September 1944. In labor unit in southern Hungary. March to Austrian border. In Austrian village. Local populace provide food. Death march. Liberation at Gunskirchen camp. Return to Hungary. Attempt of 650 Jews to reach Eretz Yisrael "illegally." Banished to Cyprus after struggle with British. In Eretz Yisrael, February 1948.

Rifles against water bottles

Our only surviving relative in Gyongyos was an aunt. The community received us nicely, but we had no desire to remain in Hungary and we decided to go to Eretz Yisrael. My brother became an active member of the Bnai Akiva religious Zionist youth movement. I joined Youth Aliya. We had a camp in a hamlet near Budapest. We were taught Hebrew and Zionism. In December 1945 we got the green light and prepared to go to Eretz Yisrael as "illegals," under the auspices of the Aliya Bet organization.

After the Budapest camp, we stayed in many other camps in Austria and Germany. The American authorities, the [American Jewish] Joint [Distribution Committee] and the UNRRA [United Nations Relief and Rehabilitation Administration] provided us with food and clothing. At the end of 1946 we reached France. There we waited a long time till we got permission to board a ship, the Negev, anchored in a port near Marseilles.

We boarded the ship in January 1947. There were about 650 of us, mostly youths. The voyage to Haifa took about four weeks. We were on the Mediterranean Sea for 27 days. It was hard. The sea was rough and the food was inadequate. At one point, the water and food supply simply ran out. We were near Sicily. The captain decided to put in at Siena, Sicily. We didn't want to risk going ashore. We collected money or valuables from everybody and gave it to two or three sailors – I don't remember whether they were Greeks or Turks – to use it to buy us provisions. They absconded with the money. In vain we waited for them for a day or two. The situation got worse and members of the crew went ashore and reported to the Coast Guard: there are refugees on the ship starving to death. The Italian Coast Guard people came and saw how dire our situation was, so they collected money – apparently donations – and brought us dried fruits, oranges and tangerines, filled our water tanks, and wished us a successful voyage. Four or five days later we were in Haifa.

A few kilometers before Haifa we had noticed two large battleships, which soon had us sandwiched between them. They sprayed us with water and threw smoke grenades at us. We refused to surrender and we threw water bottles and articles lying around on the deck back at them. A platoon of British soldiers led by an officer, equipped with batons and shields, jumped onto the deck of our ship, and the battle began. There were more of us, and we fought back in every way we could. One of the officers fired a gunburst in the air, wounding two of our group and killing one. We surrendered and went down to the ship's hold. The next day they took us ashore in Haifa. (The next "illegal" ship was named "The Unknown Illegal," after the man who had been killed.) Before that, we put the motor out of commission and wrecked everything, so that nothing on the ship should remain intact. They dragged us off the ship. Then they had to drag each and every one of us from ship to ship. That is how, in early February 1947, we were transferred to Cyprus. We were in Cyprus till January 1948, when our turn came – as part of the monthly quota of 1,500 Jews the British were permitting to enter the country. During that year in Cyprus, emissaries came from Eretz Yisrael. One of them, from Kibbutz Tirat Zvi, spent about 20 days with us – helping us, teaching us, telling us about his kibbutz, succeeding in persuading some of us to join the kibbutz. When we reached Eretz Yisrael, I and five other young men joined Tirat Zvi.

Wife: Berta

Offspring: Listed in testimony of wife, Berta Fon

Yaacov Frenkel

Born 1930 in Berettyoujfalu, Hungary. Life till German occupation. Nagyvarad ghetto. Yaakov's and other rabbinical families transferred to Budapest. Columbus camp, end of June 1944. Place becomes protected house. Budapest ghetto from early December till liberation in January 1945. Rabbi's death and burial in ghetto. Father's fate in Russian captivity at Focsani, Rumania. Zionist training camps in Hungary and Germany. To Eretz Yisrael in December 1947 after detention in Cyprus from February.

Fourteen and a half years old

The houses in the Budapest ghetto were tightly packed with families. We were one of the few families from outside the city. In the wake of the retreat of the Germans and of the Hungarian Army, the labor units also withdrew, and thousands of exhausted men arrived in the ghetto. This was to be of help to us later on. We got food from the Jewish community council's central kitchen. It was meager fare – some bread and jugs of soup. We had a hard time taking care of my brother – he was a year and three months old, and he looked no more than half a year old. We had no electricity, no heat and not enough water, and I remember us warming the baby's food with candles.

In December Budapest was completely surrounded and the city was being heavily bombarded. We had to go down to the basement along with all the other residents of the house. It was extremely crowded in the basement. During this period things deteriorated. We had to ration our food very carefully, the crowding got worse, and water was hard to come by. I was the big hero as I volunteered to bring water for us and the people near us. At this time they started piling up corpses in the yards. Some were killed in the bombardments, but most died of malnutrition and sickness. It was dangerous to go outside, and I would bring water under a rain of bombs. More than once as we stood waiting for water, bombs fell in the area and fallout dropped into the water. Sometimes a bomb fell near the entrance to the building and we had to move to a different basement through an emergency opening.

My grandfather was about 65, a spent man. Perhaps the disappointments and everything that was happening around him had knocked all the strength out of him. Back home he used to caution us to behave ourselves, saying we didn't know what was in store for us. He was with us in the basement, in the area where people lay beside each other, near the corner that served as a toilet. He could not endure it all. We woke up one morning and found him dead. Usually, the corpses were piled onto carts and hauled away. When the men from the labor unit came along – in the ghetto, some of them knew him from the time he was rabbi in Berettyoujfalu – they decided they'd find a way to bury him properly. First they took the body up to the top floor of the house. The Jewish practice is not to leave the body of a dead person unattended, so they had me stay with the body. I can't forget that night. The city was undergoing an air raid. The place had no windows or doors. The others were in the basement, and I, a boy of 14, was all alone in the house guarding a dead man, and all around me there was bombing and shelling and cold.

The Almighty was good to my grandfather through those men who had said that something had to be done to arrange a decent burial for him. Part of the basement was unpaved and partitioned into small sections to serve as storage spaces. For the time being they buried my grandfather in one of those sections. Later they removed the body and gave it a proper Jewish burial. That is how Grandpa got special treatment.

I was only 14 1/2, and I had a baby and an old grandmother with me. I find it hard today to imagine how I endured all that.

Wife:	Tzipora			
Children:	Miriam	Hannah	David	Milka
Grand-children:	Sarit	David		
	Elyakim	Sarah		
	Benaya	Berechia		
	Hodaya	Yehuda		
	Rivka			

27

Haya (Katie) Goldberger (nee Schindler)

Born 1930 in Hajdunanas, Hungary. Jewish life in Hajdunanas. Trouble because of lack of Hungarian citizenship. Mayor places father under house arrest so he shouldn't be banished from Hungary. Subsisting after father deprived of livelihood. Young Haya rebels against degrading treatment by Hungarians. To ghetto, then to Debrecen brick factory. Putting on Tefillin at Bar Mitzva despite danger. Journey in cattlecars toward Czechoslovakia and back to Strasshof. Families able to work sent to Austria. Work at Amaliendorf in factory making clothing for German Army. Father deported to Bergen-Belsen. Teresienstadt. To Hungary after liberation. Rumania. Haya's attempt to get to Eretz Yisrael from Brno with group of youths. In Germany with Dror Habonim Socialist Zionist youth group. With parents in Austria. To Eretz Yisrael from Italy with Youth Aliya, December 1947.

The rebel

When Mama decided to go to Budapest to try to earn some money to support the family, Papa became very edgy and short-tempered. The fact that Mama had to go and he was under house arrest literally made him sick.

When the yeshivot were closed, my brothers came home and our situation became even more difficult. At that time we were producing shoes of woven straw for the Hungarian and German Armies. The shoes were supposed to protect the feet against frostbite. Papa brought piles of straw. We had to weave the straw on forms.

I was a rebellious, unforgiving sort: if anyone hit me, I hit back. Papa once grabbed me and shook me, saying: "What are you doing? Do you want that Gentile whose son you spit at to come in here? Do you realize what he'll do if he comes into our house? You'll be the ruin of us!"

This worked for two or three weeks, and then again I lost control of myself. Only this time I did something very serious: I didn't pull the straw tight enough. And again the Gentile in charge complained: "Do you want the feet of our soldiers to freeze?"

Nothing dire happened to us, but we were not permitted to do that work anymore. Again I felt that I was to blame, that instead of helping I had done something wrong.

Mama stopped going to Budapest, because she saw that it made Papa sick. She bought some ducks and geese. We would slaughter them ritually, cook them and sell the smoked meat. We had some income from that and we had food, but this didn't go on for long. House searches began. This was black-marketeering, an unforgivable crime. We did it in the house between two doors, and we mailed the meat once a week to Miskolc, packed in marmalade containers, about five kilograms per container. From time to time I would bring the stuff to the post office. For a nice portion of goose liver, the clerk would turn a blind eye. There were special detectives whose job it was to look out for such illegal activities.

I remember once setting out with the boxes and seeing one of the detectives standing there watching me. I stopped and said to him: "Tell me, sir, why are you standing there staring at me? Didn't you ever see a box of marmalade before?" He knew Papa and knew that I was his daughter. He said: "Cheeky Jew! Beat it before I give you a couple of slaps." Since we did not have Hungarian citizenship, we were very much afraid. If anyone were to complain against Papa, the whole family would be deported immediately. When Papa heard what happened, he was angry again: "What do you want," he said to me, "that they should deport us?" I felt awful, but something similar happened again.

Our drinking-water supply was some distance from the house. I took water from one of the nearby courtyards, and one of the Gentile children came toward me and called out: "Dirty Jew!" I retorted: "I'm not dirty. I'm a Jew alright, but I'm not dirty!" He said: "How come you say you're not dirty? The Jews are cry-babies. Filthy and dirty!" I spilled the contents of my pitcher on him. I told Papa. "Now what have you done?" he scolded me. Poor Papa. He waited for that boy's father to show, but nothing happened. I tried to stop doing things like that.

Husband:	Yisrael		
Children:	Esther	Varda	Malka
Grand-children:	Idit		Yoel
	Yael		Yaakov
	Shmuel		
	David		
	Hadas		

Yisrael Goldberger

Born 1922 in Szatmar, Transylvania. Parents' home. Hungarians arrive, October 5, 1940. Evades draft by means of false documents. In Margareten, 1942. Returns home when Germans enter Hungary; drafted for forced labor in Ukraine, May 1944. Hungarians' cruelty in forced-labor camp at Stri-Doline, and arduous work chopping trees for fortifications. On foot to Hungary and escape, October 1944. Arrest by gendarmes at Debrecen on way to Budapest. In Budapest, shelter in protected buildings in Arena Street, 32 Benczur Street and Columbus camp. Bergen-Belsen; *Sonderlager*. To Teresienstadt by train, April 1944. Liberated by Americans at Teresienstadt, May 8, 1945. Back to Szatmar, July 1945. To Austria with help of *Briha*, Zionist underground movement taking survivors to Eretz Yisrael. Six-week military course by Hagana, Zionist underground military formation, in Hochland, Germany. To Eretz Yisrael via Austria and Italy.

30

The singer from Bergen-Belsen

From Columbus camp in Budapest we were taken to Bergen-Belsen. In the railroad station they promptly lined us up five abreast – that was their system. From the station we walked several kilometers to Bergen-Belsen. We walked through the gateway. We were all wearing ordinary clothing. They took us to a warehouse and ordered us to undress in order to put on clothes and shoes they would give us, but they didn't give us a thing. Fortunately, I was in the *Sonderlager*, a special camp in Bergen-Belsen, whose Jewish inmates were considered candidates for exchange for German subjects held in "enemy" countries. After we undressed, they ordered us to put on our clothing again. In my pocket I had my *Tefillin*, and they remained with me throughout that period. They put us in barracks – the familiar barracks of Bergen-Belsen. Every barrack was long as Exile, and from one end it was impossible to see the other end.

We began the daily Bergen-Belsen schedule. They woke us in the dark and ordered us outside for *Zehlappel* (rollcall). We stood for hours in that hellish frost, dressed in almost nothing. I had no shoes, nothing but rags covering my feet. On the first day they gave us *Gemuese* – an insipid vegetable soup. We were still finicky and didn't want to eat the soup. The SS men laughed and said that we would yet eat it. I ate it on the very first day, because I was no longer so finicky. They distributed a very carefully measured square of bread. I don't remember exactly how many people shared that bread, but there were plenty of them. The bread was also weighed, and someone devised a scale with cord at each side, lest, God forbid, someone get a slice weighing as much as a gram more than someone else got. I saved up bread to get myself shoes. I had saved up half a loaf, when it was stolen. If someone took sombody else's bread, that was a great disaster, for bread meant life.

Luckily for me, I could sing. God had blessed me with a pleasant voice, and to this day, for the past 40 years, I lead the *Mussaf* service in the High Holy Day services. In the evenings I would go from barrack to barrack singing Yiddish songs. The next day each barrack would give me a spoonful of *Gemuese*. There was a woman in the *Sonderlager* who had come from Austria with five children. She had obtained milk for the children, and she gave me some, for my singing. Later I met her in Israel.

When I got engaged, I visited my wife's relatives. She took me to an aunt of hers, my future father-in-law's sister. When we arrived, the aunt was sleeping, but her daughter, who had received us, jumped up with a shout: "The singer from Bergen!" I didn't remember her, but she had recognized me. In Bergen I had always worn a cap. She took off my fedora and put a cap on my head, saying: "Yes, that's him." She woke her mother and said: "Mama, the singer from Bergen is here!" This happened to me several times.

I think those songs had taken them back to their homes. I sang Yiddish songs that had been popular then – Sabbath songs, family melodies. In Bergen-Belsen I had several friends from our hometown. They came along on my singing rounds as my assistants. I already had assistants, and they also enjoyed part of the "fees" I collected. It may be said that that is what kept me alive. I'm sure of that, because every gram of bread there meant: life.

Wife: Haya

Offspring: Listed with testimony of wife, Haya (Katie) Goldberger

31

Baruch Gruenwald

Born 1921 in Kisvarda, Hungary. Parents' home. In Komarom for conscription into forced-labor units. Freed on medical grounds, 1942. Drafted for labor in mass conscription at Kosice, May 1943. Work at preparing huntings grounds for Horthy. Laying rail line at Kelemenhavas till summer 1944. Visits Kisvarda ghetto with permission of labor-unit commander. Meeting with father. Three weeks at Tohat. Digging trenches and bunkers at Borsa till mid-October. Avoid entering Galicia at commander's initiative. Quick march to Kosice region, home of unit commander, and release of men by Tisza. Liberated by Russians, October 26, while at Beregsom farm. Work for Hungarian farmer and return to Kisvarda. Finds father's books at home of Hungarian neighbor. With friend to Rumania, stay in Arad and Bucharest. With Bnai Akiva religious Zionist youth group from December 1945. To Eretz Yisrael, April 1946.

Messenger of mercy

At Sátor-Tábor they concentrated the Jews of the entire region – eastern Hungary, Carpatho-Russia and central Hungary. Among them were Orthodox Jews, Reform Jews, Hassidim and Neologs from age 18-19 to age 50. I was quartered with a group of non-religious Jews who enjoyed music, but I remained observant. There were some Zionists who after working hours spoke Hebrew among themselves. I clearly remember us saying that everything we did there was in preparation for life in Eretz Yisrael.

One group of 50 organized themselves to guarantee a supply of kasher food. The people in charge were agreeable, and they supplied suitable provisions. The liberal treatment we received was thanks to the Czechoslovakian-born commander. He was a World War I hero who had been conscripted for this task. About the concentration of the Jews in ghettos in April 1944 we learned from Jews returning from furloughs. Many people of the labor units wished to visit their homes, and the commander granted them leaves; that is how I got to visit my family. After traveling a whole day and night I arrived at my family's apartment in the ghetto. I was wearing my labor-unit uniform with a yellow armband and had a leave pass signed by the commander. Mama had died the previous year and Papa was left with my two sisters. He was active on behalf of the community, mainly in mobilizing food. He told me that a granddaughter had been born to the chief rabbi, Rabbi Rosenbaum, and asked me to be a holy messenger of mercy and go and get milk for the baby from a dairy farmer at the far end of town. He thought it would be simpler for me, in my labor-unit uniform, and so did I. Besides, "Those on sacred mission are not harmed," according to the old Jewish saying. I arrived at the farm about two kilometers outside town and waited about 20 minutes for the farmer to show up. He gave me milk and asked me to leave as quickly as possible. I returned to the ghetto and delivered the milk. When I left the house, two gendarmes were standing across the street. They called out to me: "What are you doing here?" I showed them my pass. They ordered me to return to my labor unit immediately. I went back into the house and kissed Papa and my sisters goodbye.

Wife:	Shoshanna		
Children:	Yehoshua*	Esther	Elisheva
Grand-children:		Shlomit	Moriah
		Efrat	Tzofiya
		Eliezer	Yitzhak
		Noam	Gilad
		Yehoshua	
		Tehilla	
		Ayala	
		Tzipora	

* of blessed memory

Sarah Kaiser (nee Schreiber)

Born Seletin, Bukovina. Year under Russian rule, 1940. Under Rumanian-German rule from June 1941; Yedinetz till September. Mogilev-Podolsk ghetto. Liberation, August 1944. To Eretz Yisrael with Youth Aliya. Cyprus, Karkur, Mikve Yisrael, Nir Galim.

Thanks to my uncle

Our family – my parents, I and my sister – lived in Seletin, a village in Bukovina containing some 300 Jewish families. The Russians entered Seletin in June 1940. In June 1941 the Rumanian and German armies came.

A few weeks later they announced that the Jews were being deported to the district capital. In the morning the Jews were summoned to the Village Hall, where the Rumanian soldiers divided them into groups – rich Jews, poor Jews, Communists. In the evening we and some other Jews were told to come to the movie theater, where we were told we were being sent to Radauti. We put whatever we could into knapsacks. Some Jews were able to take along carts. It was a two-to-three-day walk to Radauti.

In Radauti we lived with relatives for several months, until an order came that all Jews who had come to Radauti from the villages were being expelled to Bessarabia. The few people who had some money rented wagons. We, along with many other Jews, went on foot, escorted by Rumanian soldiers. It took us weeks to reach Yedinetz. There was plenty of room there. In some streets there were empty houses. I have no idea what happened to the Jews who had lived there.

While we were in Yedinetz Papa and Grandpa were conscripted by the Rumanian Army for forced labor. Grandpa was about 60 then. We didn't hear a word about them for three months. Many Jews died in Yedinetz of starvation and disease. We were there till December, when the order came expelling all the Jews there to Transnistria.

My sister remained in Czernowitz. I was now the only girl in the family. I was with my parents, with Grandpa and Grandma, and with my uncle and aunt. Again we went on foot. It was winter, and it was very cold and a heavy snow fell. At night we slept outdoors. Along the way people were shot by Rumanian soldiers. We stopped at Atakij, where we met many Jews from Bukovina. We also met the relatives with whom we had stayed. They had also been ordered to move to Transnistria.

We continued on to Mogilev. There we had an uncle, a brother of Papa's, who had a little money, and he arranged for us to stay in Mogilev. Our whole family lived in one room in the ghetto. Most of the Jews continued walking.

In Mogilev we kept ourselves alive by trading our remaining valuables for food: potatoes and flour. During our first year there Grandma died of typhus. Many Jews died of starvation and disease. Every night piles of corpses were carted out of the ghetto and dumped in pits. They were not buried. My parents and my uncle and aunt also took sick. I was the only one not to get sick. I was a girl of 10 bearing the whole burden. I brought the food from the market and I took care of all the sick people in my family. Later things eased up. Through some messengers we got a bit of money from relatives in Bucharest, and afterwards the Zionist organizations also helped. We remained in Mogilev a few months after the place was liberated by the Red Army.

We survived thanks to my uncle, Papa's brother, who had arranged for us to stay in Mogilev and shared his room and the little that he had with us. Two brothers and two sisters of Mama's had to go on to Transnistria where they perished.

Husband:	Meir			
Children:	Shlomo	Varda	Gideon	Yosef
Grand-children:	Dana	Noam	Sivan	
	Revital		Liel	
	Mattan		Bar	

35

Haya Kalla (nee Kalla)

Born 1927 in Nyirmada, Hungary. Parents' home and pre-war atmosphere. Kisvarda ghetto. Six weeks later to Auschwitz. Selection by Mengele and six weeks in Block 27. Gorlitz camp and work in factory making airplane spare parts – five months. Liberated by Russians, May 1945. Return to Hungary, June 1945. Zionist training camp in Budapest. To Israel via Cyprus, 1949. Memories of Gorlitz and Auschwitz.

Different tyrannies

From Auschwitz we were transferred to the Gorlitz camp. There were only women in the place where I was. We were there five months, till the liberation. We worked in a factory making airplane spare parts. We walked from the camp to the factory and back. We worked in shifts, each week alternating between the day and night shifts. We had to work at the machine 12 hours a day standing up. The machines were operated electrically, and we had to make and arrange the little parts for the airplanes. It was exhausting work, and we often dozed off on our feet. This was forbidden, of course. Sometimes, when we felt we couldn't go on any more, we went to the toilet, where we could sit, sometimes falling asleep there. The foreman was a German, as were the supervisors and inspectors. Whenever anything went wrong they punished us by shaving our hair or giving us a beating.

I remember one instance when one of the girls was punished for taking a potato while she was outside the camp. They made her stand before all the prisoners and they gave her an awful beating with a rod. Then they shaved her head. I don't know what finally became of her, but she looked terrible. It was hard to look at her in that condition.

A short while before the liberation they wanted to transfer us to another place, and we started walking. In our camp, as I said, there were only women. Next to our camp was a men's camp. Their commandant was a convicted criminal, a German. We heard that he was a murderer and had been transferred to the camp from prison. The men were much worse off than us. They were constantly beaten, and every day prisoners died there. They were all skin and bones. Things got worse during the march when the Germans were transferring us to another camp. It was very hard to walk. I was unable to go on walking and my cousin dragged me. I could barely drag along till we were given a chance to rest. The men marched with us. They were totally exhausted. The Germans shot them. All along the way, whenever they saw that somebody had trouble walking, they shot him. At one stop we saw that very few men were still alive. When the Russians arrived, very, very few men had survived to be liberated. Finally we stopped and went back to Gorlitz.

I remember the liberation. The Germans left. But we were still scared by the sound of the exploding shells and bombs. Some of the girls cheered us on. We were happy when the Russians came.

Husband:	Hayim		
Children:	Pinhas	Esther*	Carmit
Grand-children:	Ahimeir		
	Esther		
	Noa		
	Carmel		

* of blessed memory

Yosef Karmon (Kellner)

Born 1928 in Puspokladany, Hungary. Debrecen ghetto to Auschwitz till August 1944. Goleszow camp, satellite of Auschwitz, August 1944 to January 1945. Brunlitz camp till liberation, May 1945. Return to Puspokladany. Zionist training camps. Several arrests in course of attempts to steal across borders to Eretz Yisrael. Israel, June 1949.

Purpose to life

The Goleszow camp was a vacation resort compared to Birkenau. When we arrived, it contained Greeks and Hungarians. They said conditions had improved considerably since the beginning. There was a cement factory there. The prisoners worked in a stone quarry, delivering the stones by wagons to the factory, where they put them into furnaces and turned them into cement. Raw material was transported from there by cargo planes. We worked all week from morning before dawn till after dark. On Sundays we worked half a day, and we even got milk. Every morning and evening we got a small ration of bread, and in the afternoon we were given cooked food. We lived in a building of three or four storeys. The *kapos* were Jews and they treated us decently. The *Lageraeltester* (prisoner chief) was a German political prisoner, and his attitude was reasonable so long as we worked. There was a dispensary. Prisoners requiring complicated treatment were sent to Auschwitz. The camp was ringed by an electric fence, and nobody ever escaped. When we went off to work we were escorted by SS men.

I remember that once they killed a Jew along the way. It was a tailor who had provided the Germans with various services, asking for food in return. One day the SS man got fed up with this Jew's "pestering." He asked him to go get something and shot him. Later the SS man said he shot him because he tried to escape. I also remember a Jewish *kapo* who was very cruel. He was from Poland and a veteran prisoner. He behaved like a German. His freedom of movement allowed him to spend time with women whenever he went out of the camp.

Observing the Jewish rituals in camp, despite all the doubts that haunted you, gave purpose and meaning to life. On Yom Kippur I wanted to fast. On the morning of the day before Yom Kippur we got a bread ration. I got hold of some beet intended for the animals and ate it before the fast. I had also saved three bread rations and ate them when Yom Kippur was out.

They knew that some Jews fasted on Yom Kippur. That day the *Lageraeltester* assembled the Jews in the mess hall and forced them to eat. I managed to avoid going in there. Whenever I wanted to ritually rinse my hands before eating, I did so with the coffee water under the table in the mess hall. On Rosh Hashana Eve, the *Lageraeltester*, whose birthday it was, allowed us to hold a prayer service. Many people came. I don't know where they got a *prayerbook, but the hazzan* (prayer leader) had one. Many Jews showed up, and we all prayed and cried. We tried to do the same for the Kol Nidrei service on Yom Kippur Eve, but the chief did not have a birthday that day. They dispersed us as we were reaching the high point of the service. That night they punished those who had tried to run away. We were all lined up on the assembly ground, then they put a gallows in the middle of the assembly area, called out the names of the "culprits" and hanged them.

On Hanukka I saw a candle burning near a window. Hard to believe, but someone dared to light a Hanukka candle!

The moment I arrived at Auschwitz I asked myself, and I have ever since constantly asked myself: "Is this the lot of European Jewry? Does the Jewish people deserve such a fate?" I still ponder on this question and I have no answer. But this is a far cry from forsaking my faith.

Wife:	Leah			
Children:	Batya	Shilo	Yitzhak	Gittit
Grand-children:	Meirav	Maayan		
	Oded	Yiftah		
	Inbal			

Shlomo Lajos, *of blessed memory*

Born 1922 in Hudlova, Czechoslovakia. Satoraljaujhely before Germans enter Hungary. Ghetto. First transport to Auschwitz. From Auschwitz to Mauthausen, then to Ebensee. Liberated by Americans, May 5, 1945. Home again. Flight from Hungary to Zionist training camp in Czechoslovakia, 1946. Cyprus camps, 1947. Eretz Yisrael, 1948.

The fate of a Jewish prisoner at Ebensee

When we got to Ebensee, there were about 3-5,000 prisoners there of various nationalities: Greeks, French, Poles, Russians and Ukrainians. There were about 500 Jews, apparently the first group of Jews. Later additional transports joined us. As soon as we arrived we were met by Poles, Russians and people of other nationalities. They took our shoes and gave us wooden clogs instead. If we did not hand them over we were beaten. On the fourth day, we went to work in the quarries. There was a series of three tunnels they had dug to lay tracks for the railcarts.

A few days later we were lined up to watch three Jews being flogged to death. I don't know why. In the evening they beat us, too, and the other prisoners joined in. We were beaten steadily from 7 o'clock till midnight.

I worked in cave No. 5. Our job was to collect the waste that accumulated after the dynamitings, pile it onto the railcarts, wheel it away, dump it and return the carts to the rails for reloading. It was backbreaking work. We worked from 5 in the morning till 6 in the evening. At noon we ate a skimpy meal in the quarry. In the morning we got black coffee and in the evening coffee and one third of a breadloaf. Frequently the non-Jewish prisoners – especially the Russians and Ukrainians – on seeing a Jewish prisoner eating, grabbed the food literally right out of his mouth, and that would be the end of our meal.

At Ebensee there were no Jewish *kapos*. The *kapos* were mainly Germans. The prisoners included Czechs, French and Russians, but there were many Germans. The infirmary consisted of two barracks: a large one for non-Jewish prisoners and a small one for Jews. Once I fell and hurt myself while at work and I was sent to the infirmary for two weeks. I was looked after by an alert Jewish doctor, Dr. Levy, who extracted the pus from my foot and put a paper bandage on it.

Then I was sent to work in the small quarries, at mine 26. There I took severe beatings from the German *kapo* and my hand swelled up. The good Dr. Levy wasn't there anymore. He had been sent out to work – I suppose because he was taking too good care of the patients. It was already Succot (Feast of Tabernacles) when I recovered. The treatment of the Jews worsened. Non-Jewish prisoners got one third of a breadloaf while we got only one ninth. Just twice a week we got a quarter of a loaf. When I was well again I was sent to work in block 10. Again I was beaten and my other foot swelled up. I went into the hospital for two weeks. Luckily, I was not sent to the "convalescence" barracks, blocks 22 and 23. Block 23 was for Jews, and people did not come out of there alive. Those sent there were either poisoned or beaten to death. I was in the hospital till the Americans came in May 1945. When I came to Ebensee and throughout my stay there, I did not believe that I would get out of there alive.

Wife: Leah

Children: Hanna   Shoshanna   Atara   Haya

Grand-   Rivka   Shlomo
children: Shmuel
            Yoel
            Reuven
            Rahel

41

Leah (Eva) Landesmann (nee Schwartz)

Born 1930 in Albert-Irsa, Hungary. Antisemitism. Denied shelter in convent. Father and other public figures banished to Budapest and arrested. Calming messages from Budapest Jewish leadership. Mother punished for not sewing yellow patch on dress, tried, arrested in Monor, banished to Kistarcsa. Grim atmosphere in ghetto; attitude of local Gentiles. To Auschwitz; selection. In camp hospital. Efforts to find parents in Auschwitz. Removed by Mengele from group marked for extermination, August 1944, and put on transport to Ravensbrueck. Work in electric-cable factory. Neustadt camp. Saved from punishment by Polish woman prisoner. Death march from Neustadt and liberation by Americans. Return to Hungary. Zionist training camp and other Zionist activity till going to Eretz Yisrael, 1947.

My village Albert-Irsa

We lived in Albert-Irsa, a little village about 50 kilometers from Budapest. My father was rabbi and cantor. I was an only child, and spoiled. I attended the local Christian high school, as there was no Jewish school. Some of my teachers were nuns. We got along well with our Hungarian and Slovak neighbors until Hungary signed a pact with Germany. Then the attitude to us changed drastically. The youth wore green shirts and belonged to antisemitic organizations. Most of the adults were afraid and they didn't try to stop the youth. I had a very good friend at school, and in the period just before the Germans arrived she was afraid to be seen with me, because she was afraid of her brother, an antisemite. At first they looked for Jews who didn't have Hungarian citizenship. When things got worse, my mother started worrying about me, and she wanted me to be in the convent - the same convent where our nun teachers lived.

One day, a few months before the Germans arrived, my mother and I went to the convent and spoke to the mother superior. She refused to take me in, saying that she herself didn't have Hungarian citizenship and that four generations back she had a Jewish ancestor. She said she didn't have the right to endanger the whole convent and the nuns. We failed in our mission and we went back. We cried – I especially. I had just been reading a book about the Spanish Inquisition and I remembered the Jews who had tried to save themselves without success. I was afraid I would meet the same fate. It was hard for me, just 14, to pretend that I wasn't scared.

Meanwhile, things went from bad to worse. The newspapers wrote that the Jews were occupying positions that rightly belonged to Hungarians and that the war was all their fault. Mama racked her brain trying to think of some way.

When the German Army entered Hungary, terrible things started happening to the Jews. On March 21 they rounded up all the Jewish notables of Albert-Irsa, including my father and the owners of the big stores. We naively thought they were only being taken for a short interrogation, but they were sent to Budapest to prison. Now Mama and I had only each other. It was difficult, but the newspapers carried soothing announcements by Kastner, the editor of the Jewish newspaper and a member of the Jewish Community Council in Budapest. Shortly afterwards Mama was arrested in the village by a gendarme for not having her yellow patch on her overcoat. She had removed the patch from one coat and pinned on another one. They sent her to Monor for trial. I was now alone in the world and I went to live with a Jewish family in the village.

Some Christians in the village brought me the last letter I ever got from Papa. It had been written about the time we were herded into the ghetto. He wrote that he loved us, and that we should obey orders and not worry, "everything is going to be all right." Later I learned that he was sent to Sopron and then to Auschwitz. Mama's letter reached me by accident. One day some Christians from the village passed by the ghetto fence. When they saw me, they laughingly told me they had got a letter from my mother. I had been eagerly looking forward to this letter and praying that it should come already, and it hadn't even occurred to them to bring it to me. I asked: "Why didn't you bring me the letter? It was addressed to me, not you!" Then they gave me the letter. It seems she had sent it through them thinking that was the only way it would reach me. That's how I found out that after the trial at Monor, Mama was sent to prison in Kistarcsa.

Husband: Bezalel

Children:	Sarah	Gila	Irit	Dorit	Efrat	Yaacov

Grand-children:	Sahar	Moshe	Noa	Ari
	Orr	Sagi	Ya'ir	Nehora
	Magen	Elad	Tamar	Henia
	Meishar	Pinhas	Barak	

Great-grand-child: Rivka

David Leitner

Born 1930 in Nyiregyhaza, Hungary. Father conscripted into labor units, 1940, 1941, 1942. Attitudes of local populace and Slovak neighbors. Ghetto and Nyirjes camp. To Auschwitz, end of May or early June. Gypsy camp in Birkenau. Children to Camp E after Gypsy camp liquidated. In *Scheisskommando* (latrine squad) till *Sonderkommando* revolt, October 7, 1944. Mengele removes 51 children, including David, from crematorium number 5. Unloading potatoes. March to Althammer. Mauthausen camp. March to Gunskirchen; conditions there. Return to Hungary. To Eretz Yisrael, 1949.

How they were ransomed

In Birkenau the barracks were in the charge of *Blockaelteste* (block chiefs). They were generally non-Jewish Poles, with assistants. Every one of them had a boy or two of whom he was very fond – to serve him and perhaps for other purposes about which we had no inkling then. They didn't want "their" boys to be selected for the gas chambers, so each one saw to ransoming "his" boy.

How did they ransom them? They would go into the barracks and indiscriminately pick children to be sent to the gas chamber instead of "their" boys.

Once, on the day before the Simhat Torah holiday, some block chiefs came to snatch children. Not many were left, as most of them had been sent off in the first two selections. I was one of those seized for dispatch to the crematorium. It was impossible to escape, since they had locked us in a sealed barrack. Those – including me – slated for extermination in the third selection, scheduled for Simhat Torah, were herded into blocks 11 and 13.

Several hundred of us – all children – marched out of block 11 toward the crematorium. It was midday. I don't remember whether SS men escorted us. Oh, yes – there *was* an SS man, an awful Ukrainian by the name of Bartsky. They hadn't come out of block 13 yet. The selection was going on in there. The stronger ones were sent back inside and the rest marched to the crematorium, behind us. We walked. They took us inside and ordered us to strip naked. Of course, we knew what they intended to do with us. We stood there naked.

An order came and we were told to wait. It seems that more fit children were needed, and there was an order to select 50 of us. I was among the 50 children they took. There must have been about a thousand children inside the crematorium building. All of us were Jews from Hungary and Transvylvania and possibly also Czechoslovakia, from the areas that had been annexed to Hungary. There were 50 of us, and another one managed to join us. He had been with me in the *Scheisskommando*, the labor platoon that cleaned the latrines and sometimes also served the underground by delivering materials and information from camp to camp. He was short but healthy. I don't know how he got to be Number 51.

When the selection was over we were stood to the side. We stood there naked, wondering what they were going to with to us. We thought they might be taking us to bring wood to the crematorium, or to turn us into soap. They drove us naked outside and shoved the others inside, into the crematorium. They used their truncheons on us. Then the SS men and the *kapo* brought us clothing to put on and walked us back to the camp. I think that that Simhat Torah, that Day of the Rejoicing Over the Torah, we all rejoiced, even the antisemitic Polish Gentiles, for that was the first time that anyone had ever come back from the crematorium alive.

Of course, afterwards we kept looking for the children in whose place we had been taken to the crematorium. I remember one block chief's telling me and another child, I think not maliciously: "You see? When God wants it, you're saved."

I saw this as a kind of apology; maybe there was a bit of humanity in that *Blockaeltester*.

Wife:	Sarah	
Children:	Zehava	Erela
Grand-children:	Yishai	Irit
	Moriah	Omer
	Yohai	Yael
	Yardena	Yonatan
	Moledet	

Aviva Liebeskind (nee Rakovsky)

Born 1931 in Bratislava, Czechoslovakia. In Bratislava till summer 1944. From Sered camp to Auschwitz, then Freiberg camp. Work in aircraft factory till April 1945. In Mauthausen camp till liberation in May. Return to Bratislava. Bnai Akiva religious Zionist youth movement training camp, 1946. Eretz Yisrael, 1947.

After the liberation

At the time of the liberation I was in the Mauthausen camp. I don't remember many details of the liberation. We were liberated by the Americans. I remember that there were Jewish soldiers among them. I could speak a little English and I told one of the soldiers about what we had undergone. I remember how shocked he was by what I told him and he brought me chocolate, which was very expensive there at that time. I remember how hungry we were at the time of the liberation.

Shortly afterwards they took our group by freighter to Bratislava. Most of the survivors on the boat were from Bratislava and all over Slovakia. When I arrived I didn't know where or to whom to go. I was almost certain that my parents weren't alive. At Auschwitz we had heard that adults with children were the first sent to the crematorium.

When I got off the boat I recognized a Jew for whom my uncle used to work. He had come there when he heard that camp survivors were on their way. I asked him if he knew anything about any of my relatives, and he said: "Yes, they're here in town!" We went there, but the doors were locked. The Russians had been in Bratislava and people were scared, and they didn't go out after dark. I remember them looking down at us from the upper floor when we went up the stairs and rang the doorbell, and the shocked look on their faces when they saw me. I looked terrible. I was down to 38 kilograms and very skinny, full of sores and dressed in tatters. I stayed with those relatives a few days. The food was very skimpy. Then they took me to the home of other relatives in the countryside. I was famished, and they fed me day and night. They cautioned me to eat in small amounts, and I ate with breaks of several hours between meals, during the day and at night. Over the summer I gained 20 kilos. All this time I suffered from sores. I was hospitalized when a big sore appeared on my head. I wanted to study. I attended school for about a year, but it didn't work. I had a very hard time applying myself to learning. The high school was a four-year school, and I was in the second year when I quit. When I came back, I went right into the second year without having learned the earlier material, so there was a big gap in my background.

In 1946 I joined a Bnai Akiva training camp. I didn't know a soul there. I was told where to find the Bnai Akiva office and I went and signed up. There I formed ties with people my age, many of whom had, like me, lost their parents in the Holocaust. In 1947 we went to Eretz Yisrael as "illegal immigrants," on forged papers saying we were demobilized Czech soldiers. We had fake names, and we were attached to "parents" – adults traveling on forged papers, like us. We got a big kick out of that – every one of us had a new name and supposed parents. We had no problems landing. After spending a day with some relatives, I joined my group and we went to the Mikve Yisrael farm school.

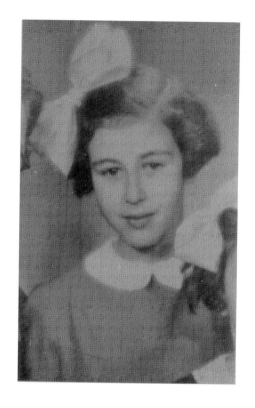

Husband:	Tzvi, of blessed memory			
Children:	Yosef	Ze'ev	Rahel	Kalman
Grand-children:	Osnat	Binyamin	Naama	
	Tzvi	Re'ut	Hagai	
		Avigayil	Tsvia	
		Nehama	Yaara	
		Hadassah		
		Tzvi		

Shmuel Nesher (Adler)

Born 1924 in Satoraljaujhely, Hungary. Details about town: Tora scholars, congregations, charitable institutions, schools. Parents' home. Attitude of Hungarians to Jews. Youth movements. Germans enter Hungary, March 19, 1944. Ghetto established. Deported to Auschwitz. Chopping down trees in Kittlitzstreben camp. Russians approach – weak people remain in camp, stronger ones taken on march. Liberated by Russians. In Heinau. Russians' attitude to liberated people. Lignitz camp for Slovaks. 28 Hungarian SS men seized in Lignitz. Vicissitudes on way to Hungary. In Satoraljaujhely and Budapest. First Zionist training camp in Hungary. Persuading Jews to go to Eretz Yisrael. Set out for Eretz Yisrael via Austria. In infirmary in Gnadenwald and Italy. From Venice by ship to Eretz Yisrael. Deported to Cyprus detention camp. Liberated. To Eretz Yisrael on s.s. Galila.

Conversation with the Almighty

The *Lageraeltester* at Kittlitzstreben was a convicted German criminal. You can well imagine how a person serving time for murdering his wife and two little children treated Jews. When he got into one of his sadistic moods, he would grab the first Jew unlucky enough to happen his way and beat him unconscious with his club. He would then pour water on him, reviving him, and then again beat him unconscious, again pour water on him, and again beat him. More than once I saw Jews die from the man's beatings. When he caught a Jew praying he would lay into him with his club. "You got nobody to believe in!" he would scream. "You got nobody to depend on! We're the lords and masters here!"

At Kittlitzstreben I worked at chopping down trees in the forest. We walked about an hour to the forest and about an hour back to camp. I used the time to say the prayers I knew by heart: the *Kriat Shma*, *Shmoneh Essray*. Then I usually carried on a conversation with the Blessed Holy One.

I asked the Blessed Holy One: "Tell me, what did we do to deserve this? What is our sin? How are we worse than any other nation? Is it because we wouldn't go to Eretz Yisrael?" And I told the Blessed Holy One the story about the Rebbe of Koznitz, who said: Because we don't know how to pray right.

The Rebbe related:

The Russian Tsar was waging a war against an enemy, and the Crown Prince was participating in that war. A soldier saw an enemy coming with his sword drawn to kill the Crown Prince, and he jumped in front of the horse and chased him away. The enemy's sword missed the mark and the Crown Prince was saved. The Tsar summoned the soldier and said to him: "Listen, soldier, you saved the Crown Prince's life. Ask for whatever you want and I'll give it to you." The soldier said: "I'm in Battalion X. The battalion commander is a bad man. Couldn't you please transfer him to another battalion?" The Tsar said: "You fool! Why don't you ask me to transfer *you* to another place and make *you* commander?" It's the same with us Jews. We are always praying to God to move us from one king to another: if there is a country that has a good king, move us to that country. We don't know how to pray right – that is our problem: we don't pray for the Redemption. Is that why we've got all this coming to us?

Do you mean to say, Master of the Universe, that ours is the worst generation ever? Do we really deserve such treatment, Master of the Universe? What is it You want? – Do You want to exterminate the Jewish People? Now I'm talking about myself. I'm not asking You, Master of the Universe, to satiate me with food. All I ask is that You bring us the Redemption. I'm not asking You to give me easier work. Just give me the strength to bear it!! That's all I ask."

That was my daily prayer: "May our eyes behold Your merciful return to Zion;" and: "Return us to You and we will return; renew our days as of old;" and: " Guardian of Israel, save the remnant of Israel." Prayer from the heart. Saying those prayers today isn't as meaningful as it was then. Only Jews in such a dire predicament can fully appreciate their significance.

Wife:	Shoshanna		
Children:	Hanna	Tzivia	Yitzhak
Grand-Children:	Shlomit	Dov	Naftali
	Efraim	Efrat	Devora
	Yigal	Noam	
	Yehuda	Elazar	
	Ya'ir	Yael	
	Naama	David	

49

Ruth Netzer (nee Gottlieb)

Born 1929 in Orkucany, Czechoslovakia. Only Jewish family in Orkucany. Expelled to Kosice after Hungarian annexation on grounds that father is Hungarian. Father detained in Garany camp because of lack of Hungarian citizenship. Zionist youth flee from Kosice to Budapest. Cousins flee to Czechoslovakia after Germans enter Hungary. To Auschwitz. Month in Bergen-Belsen, autumn 1944. To Markleeberg labor camp near Leipzig. Work in camp and in factory for airplane spare parts. Released from infirmary with help of Jewish doctor. Evacuated from Markleeberg. Hides in barn, arrested by German police. In camp for Russian women prisoners till liberation. Return to Kosice. Zionist training camp and Zionist activity till journey to Israel, 1949.

The compassion of Jewish women

I was in Bergen-Belsen about a month. In the middle of October they rounded up our group and took us to Markleeberg, a town not far from Leipzig. In this camp (a sub-camp of Buchenwald) in the Leipzig industrial zone there were only women. A group of Jewish women prisoners from Auschwitz had preceded us here, and we were followed a little later by the group that had remained in Bergen-Belsen. It was a small camp. I can't give an exact estimate of the number of prisoners, but there must have been about a thousand women.

At the outset, we didn't work in the factory near the camp. We were kept in a barrack to make sure we weren't carrying any disease and we worked inside the camp. In the camp we were guarded by SS people – SS women, but also men. There was a factory producing airplane spare parts. Later our group was assigned to work there. I didn't work in this factory, but my friend did. The workers had to stand at the machine for many long hours turning out a certain quota of parts. The workers included German civilians, and prisoners – Russians, Poles, Dutch and perhaps other nationalities. They were in a separate camp, and we met only in the factory.

At first I worked in the *Baukommando*, the construction unit. Our work consisted mainly of filling wheelbarrows with sand and hauling the loads from place to place, under the vigilant supervision of SS women. We worked in pairs – one girl would fill up the wheelbarrow and the other would wheel it from place to place. I was the youngest, and I had a hard time hauling the wheelbarrow. My partner tried to make it easier for me by not filling our wheelbarrow. The SS woman noticed. I don't remember if I got slapped, but we were warned not to do it again. After that I had to haul full wheelbarows all over the place, and it was very hard for me. After one day's work I fell sick. When work ended I came down with a high fever and I was put in the infirmary.

There was a Jewish woman doctor there, a member of our group of prisoners. She took very good care of me, but it was a long time before my fever went down. I was there nearly a month, and I was in very weak condition. From time to time SS men came to check up on the patients. One day that doctor said to me: "You shouldn't stay here. It's dangerous to be in a place like this too long. The SS officer has been coming here too frequently, and I'm afraid they're planning something."

Shortly afterwards we were all called out to a lineup, which the sick people also had to attend. One of the SS men demanded 10 women for work. The work was in the big kitchen of the factory, involving peeling potatoes. That doctor recommended me for the job. There were about 15 of us. Much to our luck, the person in charge of the kitchen was a German civilian, and we were not under the regular watch of the SS women. He and his wife treated us very decently. The place was warm and I didn't go hungry. The job I got thanks to that doctor saved my life, because my health had deteriorated, and there I gradually came back to myself.

Husband: Shmuel

Leah Feierstein (nee Stern)

We worked and prayed

We were religious, and there may have been a few more pairs of religious twins. We wanted very much to remember our Judaism, because it was our faith and we had the strength to think about it. We thought we had probably done something wrong and we accepted our fate. We said that it couldn't be that God wouldn't help us.

Some men prisoners brought food to Camp C, and they learned that we were twins. After they had been in our camp, someone went over to them, and we discovered that he was an uncle of ours. We worked at the place where they sorted the clothing, the food and the packages that the people coming on the transports brought along. When the prisoners who distributed the food came, they asked us if we needed or wanted anything, what food we wanted. We didn't want any food. We wanted a prayerbook; this was very important to us. And we got one... It never entered our mind to doubt. We were missing something. We had changed, of course, but we had not become freethinkers. We thought: we'll go home and meet Mama and the kids. We didn't want to become irreligious. Faith helped us, and we also prayed. Some twins there weren't religious. To this day they recall – whenever we meet – that we taught them to pray and had prayed together with them.

We tried our best to observe the Jewish holy days, Yom Kippur. Almost every day was Yom Kippur. We tried not to eat or drink anything for half a day. We worked and prayed.

Twin sisters Leah and Hedva. Born 1930 in Bekescsaba, Hungary. Lived in various places. Parents' home in Bekescsaba. Orthodox and Neolog communities. Community helps refugees from Poland. Ghetto established, Jewish quarters sealed off. Tobacco factory. Suicide of wealthy Neolog Jews after arrest by gendarmerie. In cattle cars to Auschwitz. Selection and transfer with twin sister to Revir. Examinations and experiments under Mengele's supervision. At Ravensbrueck and Malkov. Liberated in Germany, May 1945. Back to Bekescsaba. Zionist training camp in Budapest. To Eretz Yisrael aboard s.s. Providence, 1947.

Leah
Husband: Yaacov

Children:	Nehama	Dov	Shlomo	Zehava	Tzilla
Grand-children:	Avraham	Uriel	Moshe	Tzipora	Yael
	Rafael	Tzofia	Dvora	Batsheva	Baruch
	Sara	Noa	Yosef	Hagit	
	Yisrael	Rivka	Yoel	Menahem	
	Elazar	Milka	Yisrael		
		Moshe			
		Ruth			

Hedva
Husband: Ze'ev

Children: Shlomo Shmuel Avner Kalman

Grand-
children: Haya   Yiska   Yoel   Meir
         Yehoshua Michal Naama Sarah
         Tzvi   Naava   Rivka
         Nehama   Eliezer
         Sarah
         Miriam
         Shulamit

Hedva Katz (nee Stern)

Mama

We heard shouts: "Are there any twins here?" Mama looked at us and hugged us even tighter. She asked: "Why? What for?" They said: "Twins will have it good." She said to us: "I'm not giving you up. You're coming with me." She wanted us with her.

We moved forward till we reached somone very impressive and tall. It was Dr. Mengele. He hit people with a whip. We walked on and sort of turned left. We went forward a step or two. Mama decided to hand us over. She turned back and gave us to Dr. Mengele. The parting was very hard for us. We even got hysterical – we screamed and cried for her. Mama gestured to us with her hand and shouted: "Don't worry, you'll be following us..." Those last words of hers keep ringing in my ears to this day.

I can imagine the reason for her sudden change of mind: the tone of a Jewish mother, especially a woman already experienced in a widow's life. In order for us to have the best that was possible, she had decided to hand us over, so that we should have it good, since they had promised that twins would have it better.

Shoshanna Ofer Schwartz (nee Shirman)

Born 1924 in Hangony, Hungary. Relations with Hungarians in Hangony before and after German arrival. Deported from Ozd ghetto to Auschwitz, June 1944. Sent with group of women from Hungary via Stutthof to forced-labor camp in Grodno, together with women from Riga, August 1944. Cruelty of Ukrainian guards. Botten camp, December 1944-January 1945. Death march to Leienburg. Pause in Lodz, April-May 1945. Return to Hungary. To Israel, March 1949.

Sisters

Exhausted and starving we were packed into a freight train and we set out from Auschwitz for Stutthof. There we were kept under horrendous conditions for about three weeks. We didn't do a thing there except suffer, starve and be beaten for no reason whatever. After three weeks they transferred us in open train wagons to a place called Botten. There they quartered us in a granary. We slept on the floor, which was carpeted with straw. During the day we worked for the German army. We dug anti-tank ditches and trenches for the soldiers. It was back-breaking work. We went from early morning till well into the night without enough to eat and practically naked. The sanitary conditions there were such that we were crawling with lice.

After about two months we left Botten. Again we travelled by train, this time to Grodno. There we had to maintain and guard the tents of a Hitler Youth encampment. We piled earth around every tent, to keep it from blowing away. We worked in Grodno till January 1945 in conditions like those under which we had worked at Botten.

We set out from Grodno for Germany on foot. My sister and I had been together all along, and we were together on this march, too. I very much wanted to stay alive. We got no food during the march. In order to survive we stole food wherever we could along the way. From morning till night we walked through villages and towns whose names I no longer remember. Many of the marchers were killed along the way. If anyone got tired and sat down, they were shot on the spot.

My sister and I held hands all along the way, so that we should keep going together. We had decided to stay alive in order to look after our younger brothers. We didn't know then that they had gone up in smoke in Auschwitz.

At night we slept in barns, granaries – wherever we happened to stop. During the march my toes froze. I took off my shoes and wasn't able to put them on again. I decided not to continue, despite my sister's pleadings. At night Mama, of blessed memory, came to me in a dream and told me not to remain, to go on because we would soon be liberated. I let myself be dragged on together with my sister.

My sister was stronger than me, and she always tried in every possible way to get food. Whenever she was caught stealing food in the villages we passed through she was beaten. One day after getting a terrific beating she came crying that she couldn't take it any more and was staying behind. As I mentioned, we had resolved to get home again, because we felt responsible for our younger brothers, so this time I was the one who dragged *her*. I didn't let her stay behind. Today it's hard to figure out how we managed to stay alive. I don't think we'd have survived if we hadn't helped each other and dragged each other along and encouraged each other.

After a march of about three weeks we reached a place called Leienburg. In the camp there we didn't do a thing but lie sick. We were unable to lift a foot. I don't remember anything about life in that camp. After we were there a while – I don't remember how long – they collected all those who could still walk, including my sister, and they started walking in an unknown direction. I saw my sister through the window, moving off into the distance and screaming: "God won't forgive me for leaving my sick sister behind!" I thought to myself: "This is the end."

Husband:	Yisrael	
Children:	Penina*	Yosef*
Grand-	Vered	Yael
children:	Ayelet	Avraham
	Aviad	Hadas
	Chen	Yohai
		Devora

*Children of her husband Avraham Ofer, of blessed memory

55

Shalom Reichman, *of blessed memory*

Born 1919 in Mezokovacshaza village, Hungary. Jewish life in area. Conscripted into Hungarian Army cavalry, then to labour units. In Munkacs, Nagybanya, Sasregem. Discharged, re-conscripted at Margitta. Work in Budapest area. Assigned to east. In Scole region till September 1944. March toward Austrian border. Work at Nagykaniza till March 1945. Death march toward Mauthausen. Liberated at Gunskirchen. Return to Mezokovacshaza. Bnai Akiva religious Zionist youth movement training camp. To Israel, 1948.

The liberation

We were liberated at Gunskirchen early in May. The first moments of the liberation – that is a story in itself. I almost lost my life then. Right after the liberation my friend and I saw people helping themselves to margarine, synthetic honey, bread. My friend said that we should go grab some for ourselves, only whoever carried bread in the open was taking a chance. People pounced on you and everybody got filthy in the mud – you, those who pounced on you, the bread, and nobody got to eat it.

A few days before the liberation I removed a knapsack from somebody who had died and found toothpaste in it. That was a good thing. I and my friend licked it several times a day, to have a good taste in our mouths. I made a deal to give away the knapsack in exchange for half a sugar beet, only the knapsack was taken but I never got the sugar beet. In the early days of the liberation my friend sent me to "get something too." I saw people attacking the warehouses and stockrooms. I took my knapsack and went foraging. I found a supply of sugar beet and filled my knapsack with it. Then I found salt. What a find – salt! A very important item. You could get anything in exchange for salt. I filled both pockets with salt. In the stockrooms I found a German army coat and a duffel bag, which I also filled with pieces of sugar beet. As I headed back, some Jew came toward me carrying a gun. It seems that the departing Germans had left some weapons behind, and some of the Jews had helped themselves to guns. He came toward me: "What have you got there?" I said: "Here, you want it? Take it." I left him all my treasures. When I got back my friend yelled at me: "Everybody else brings margarine, sugar – and you?!..." I went back for another try.

In the course of these searches I found sugar. There were stockrooms of sugar, mountains of sugar. I immediately sensed that it was sugar, as I had been a grocer in Hungary. I took some and tasted it. Sugar! And I immediately started eating. Suddenly I took hold of myself: "What are you doing? We've been liberated! Why are you pouncing on the sugar that way?" I found a small towel and filled it with two kilograms of sugar, and then I tied up the towel and hid it under the sugar beet, so no one should see it. My friend said: "That's all you brought?! Why didn't you dump the beet and bring sugar instead?" I went back to bring more sugar. This time there was a mob there, only the sugar sack wasn't open. It was like when a fire breaks out inside a house, and everybody charges the door to try to break out, only the door opens inward, so they can't open it. It was impossible to open the sugar sack, because nobody would let go of it. I said: "Get off the sack! Let's lift it up! Let's open it!" Nobody would budge. I was almost trampled to death. I said to myself: "To hell with the sugar, we're free! I don't want to die now!" There was no place for me to budge, but somehow – I don't know how – I mustered all my strength and managed to get out from under the mountain of people covering me.

The sugar I brought came in handy. We had something to eat. Only the next day we were very thirsty, and there was no drinking water in the camp. There was a filthy brook, but no water to drink. We traded a cup of sugar for half a cup of water – which had to do for my friend and me.

Wife:	Rahel		
Children:	Hanna	Dov	Rivka
Grand-children:	Galit	Eliasaf	Mordechai
	Meirav	Nadav	Neriah
	Haya	Bat-Ami	Nirit
	Shiran	Avigal	Baruch
		Dikla	Shlomit
		Rotem	Moriah

Shmuel Roth

Born 1919 in Sziget, Transylvania. Conscripted into labour unit, 1941. With unit in Munkacs. Relations between Jews of Budapest and rural Jews, and with Hungarian command. Hungarian officer's antisemitism and his removal after contact between commanding officer and Budapest Jewish Community Council. Witnesses liquidation of Polish Jews at Drohobycz. Hungarian Jews' reaction to his report. Jewish woman murdered by Germans buried at commanding officer's initiative. Efforts to avoid being sent to Ukrainian front. Events in Drohobycz, April 1943: hundreds of labor-unit members die in arson attempt. Service as cook in unit of Hungarian and German officers. Gets out of march toward Austria. Famine in Budapest ghetto during fighting of January 1945. To Israel via Cyprus detention, 1949.

The officer who sided with us

There were various kinds of Hungarian officers. Some were sadists, whose cruelty is indescribable. Fortunately, our commanding officer was a refined person. I had a cousin in Munkacs. One evening I went to visit her, and came back at 12 midnight. This officer had come to make a checkup and saw me arriving. He asked me where I had been. I didn't have a pass, and it was forbidden to leave the camp without a pass. I said to him: "My cousin lives here in Munkacs, and I heard she's sick, so I went to see her." He said: "You're lucky: if the rest of them weren't asleep, I'd have given you a couple of slaps that would have made you remember me the rest of your life." He let me off without anything. Why am I telling all this? To show his attitude. It may be said that he treated us like a father. And since the commander was a good, brave man, the other members of the command staff couldn't just do as they pleased.

I was the unit's chief cook, and he – I don't know why – liked me a lot.

After we had seen the murder of Polish Jews by the Germans in Drohobycz, one of the sergeants called us all out to the assembly area. The commander arrived, and showed us a girl's hand, which a dog had found and brought over. The hand was still fresh. You could tell by the fingrnails that it was a girl's hand. He said: "Look, today is Sunday. For me this is a religious holy day, but we're allowed to work; not like with you people. We have to find the place from which this hand was taken. If anybody wants to go look – I'm ready to go along with you." We agreed, of course. We broke up into small groups and went searching. Finally we found a communications trench about 50 meters long, one of many trenches in the area, and that is where we found the bodies. It was the hand of one of the girls the Germans had murdered there three or four days earlier.

The corpses were covered by two or three centimeters of earth, and we worked till long after dark to bury them one meter deep. He wanted us to mark the place with a cross, but we decided not to do so. All we did was put a marker saying that "people" were buried there.

I came home and reported that Jews were being executed. They simply refused to believe me. They reacted coldly, as though to say: "It won't happen to me! That's not going to happen to me!"

Another story: Shortly before the Russians routed the Hungarians and Germans in December 1942, we were ordered to go to the Ukraine via the Czech border. We arrived at Gilanta. Our officer knew what going to the front would mean for us. There were some Jewish doctors in our unit, and we decided on the following stratagem: We would cause our unit to seem to have a typhus epidemic, so we would be quarantined. How? Five of us – including me – drank coffee with a lot of salt, which caused us all to have fever. And five men coming down with a fever is cause to suspect typhus. When the mayor of Gilanta refused to let us enter the city, the commander said to him: "Give me a note signed by you allowing me to proceed and cause the infection of thousands of Hungarian and German soldiers." The mayor refused to sign, so we were in quarantine in Gilanta for a month and a half. Our fevers disappeared after a day. But orders are orders: people with typhus have to be in quarantine, and, just to make sure, for a month and a half.

Wife:	Malka	
Children:	Miriam	Eliezer
Grand-children:	Tzilla	Hayim
	Gilad	Yoav
	David	Ehud
Great-grand-children:	Yoav	
	Merav	

Eliezer Safar

Born 1924 in Derecske, Hungary. Jewish life in Sagujfalu village. To Szecseny ghetto, April 1944. With labor unit in Ozd. At metal-soldering plant till June-July 1944. Clearing ruins in Budapest till October. Political coup, October 15. Weapons training till investigation by Hungarian Army and SS. Five of 10 accused young men executed. Leaves Budapest for Austria. Escape and attempt to hide in Sagujfalu. Report to military authorities in Szecseny, court martial at Miskolc. In non-Jewish unit. Prison evacuees. Another failed escape attempt. March to Sopron. Building fortifications across Austrian border. Death march to Mauthausen, March 1945. Foot hurt in bombing at Graz. In hospital as wounded Hungarian soldier, April-November 1945. Return to Hungary. Zionist training camps. To Eretz Yisrael and expulsion to Cyprus, 1948. Attitude to Holocaust.

The turning point

In January 1948 we set out from Italy for Eretz Yisrael aboard the s.s. Etzion Bloc 35. There were about 280 of us "illegals" on board. I got to Israel only in December 1948, aboard the s.s. Hatikva, after detention in Cyprus.

More than 30 years had passed since I came to Israel and I had hardly spoken about the Holocaust. Not among friends and not even in the family circle. I had taken a vow of silence, which I find hard to explain. This is not to say that the horror of those days didn't constantly haunt us and affect our day-to-day behavior. Many a time the subject came up and I was asked what had happened to my foot in the Holocaust. I always answered briefly and quickly changed the subject.

I started opening up four or five years ago, and ever since I speak about it a great deal, and write about the Holocaust in the moshav bulletin and read books on the subject – none of which I had previously been able to do.

I have tried to explain my silence to myself. Maybe it stems from the fact that we came to Israel when the War of Liberation was over, and came – it may be said – to something ready. We regarded as heroes those who had fought for the establishment of the state. We, the Holocaust survivors, tried to get ourselves swallowed into the community and to contribute whatever we could without drawing attention to ourselves and to what we had undergone. It should also be remembered that we were very preoccupied with our struggle to be allowed to establish our own settlement, form our own settlement group, and pick our own site. Finally, we had come here with nothing at all, because the Jewish Agency had helped us with only a pittance, and all our energies were taken up with developing the place. Only afterwards were we able to think about establishing families. Another reason for the ultimate opening-up, the over-riding one, was the realization that it was the duty of the survivors to tell, to write down, everything they had undergone – first, so that it should not be forgotten; secondly, to refute the malicious attempts to deny that the horrors had ever taken place.

My father, Reb Moshe, and my sister Haya reached Israel in 1951. At last we were all home – that is, all three of us who had survived from our pre-war family of 10.

In May 1953 I married Sarah, nee Eckstein, who was born in Sarvar, Hungary. Sarah and her twin sister, Leah, are also Holocaust survivors. They were among the "Mengele twins" who in Auschwitz were subjected to all kinds of horrible medical experiments conducted by that fiend Mengele. Freed, they found shelter in a convent, where their lives were saved, and when the war was over they returned to Hungary when they were only eight or nine years old. They were in a children's home, and were brought to Eretz Yisrael from the town of Deszk, also via Cyprus, in 1946. They completed their education at the Youth Aliya boarding school in Kfar Batya.

With Sarah's help and thanks to her, we have a warm home and a fine family – not a big one, but a united one. Both of us didn't talk about it, even to each other, and today we rather regret not having spoken to our children about it when they were growing up.

We have three children – a son and two daughters. All three – our son, Yitzhak, and Hanni and Raheli have done full military service in the Israel Defense Forces, the army of the sovereign state of Israel. I see this as more than symbolic, as proof that as much as our Nazi oppressors slaughtered Jews mercilessly, destroying most of our family in the process, they did not completely succeed. We are alive and well, and the Jewish people is free in its own country, and with God's help will continue to live here securely forever.

Wife:	Sarah		
Children:	Yitzhak	Hanna	Rahel
Grand-children:	Adam	Miriam	Yanir
	Hed	Adi	
		Maya	

Sarah Safar (nee Eckstein)

Born 1938 in Sarvar, Hungary. Deported to Auschwitz. Few memories of period – together with twin sister – under Mengele's supervision and medical experiments performed on them. In convent at Kattowice, Poland. From convent to Hungary with help of Jewish woman from Budapest who took them under her wing. Youth Aliya institution in Deszk. Eretz Yisrael, 1946. Youth Aliya boarding school at Kfar Batya. Marries and joins Moshav Nir Galim, 1953. Reunion with Margit Weiss, woman who took sisters from Kattowice convent.

Children as medical guinea pigs

It is hard to believe that I was part of a nightmarish scene that would not occur even to a sick imagination. In the midst of all the other horrors of Auschwitz to see children – including very small children – standing for hours in a *Zehlappell* (rollcall lineup), sometimes sitting on stools, like in kindergarten – children aged six to eight. Children snatched from their mothers' arms by Mengele, who with a swing of his hand, right or left, determined whether people were to live or die. This operation, called *Selektzie* (selection), was carried out amid inhuman shouts and roars. Only later did we learn that Mama and all those on the left had been sent to the gas chamber.

One doctor there immediately had his eye on us, as we were twins, and were candidates for the medical-scientific experiments Mengele was conducting in order to learn how to improve the German race.

The experimental barrack was called *B Lager* (Camp B). It was a long barrack filled with triple-tiers of bunks. Each bunk contained three children. We had to curl up for lack of space. I remember that the girl in the bunk with me and my sister got kicked whenever we tried to straighten our legs. In the middle of the barrack was a big stove. There were about 100 twins in the barrack. Our group included a family of midgets, though they were in a separate room.

Among the horrible things that happened, there was the shocking case of the woman who gave birth. After the baby, a girl, was born, they experimented to see how long she would survive without food and drink, until finally, a woman doctor (a Jew) ended the baby's suffering with a lethal injection.

They tattooed numbers on our arms, and from time to time they took us to the infirmary to conduct various experiments on us. They gave us all kinds of injections, put drops in our eyes, repeatedly checked our blood. The food was very skimpy: insipid soup, bread – the breadloaf was shaped like a brick – and black coffee. We would stand in the fenced-in yard watching skeleton-like people in striped clothing trudging around hauling the corpses on litters. The air was always filled with the stench of bodies burning in the crematorium not far from there.

Some children had their mothers nearby. The others were very jealous, because all of us desperately wanted our mothers. Today I realize how hard it must have been, in that hell, for those mothers to see what their children were undergoing. I came down with typhus and I was put in isolation. All I did all day was crush the lice and bugs on the wall near my bunk.

I recovered. One day I heard that we were free to go. We started walking. The younger children were placed in a convent at Kattowice.

Out of the 2,000 walkers who had been freed, many died along the way. It was rumored that there were Jewish orphans at that convent and relatives or acquaintances were allowed to take children out of there.

A certain fine woman took me and my twin sister, despite her illness. She was called "Margit Nanni." She rescued us from hell. She looked after the two of us – utterly spent and completely bald as we were. From the moment we laid eyes on her we clung to her for the next few weeks till, together with her, we completed the long route back to Hungary.

Husband: Eliezer

Offspring: Listed with testimony of husband, Eliezer Safar

63

Rahel Shemer (nee Weiss)

Born 1931 in Budapest. Parents' home. Orphanage in Budapest. Germans arrive. In marked building together with mother. Death march from Budapest. Rescued by Austrian Nazi; returns to Budapest with him. Budapest ghetto. Liberated by Russians, January 18, 1945. Racoczy Institute – Bnai Akiva religious Zionist youth movment, training camp. To Eretz Yisrael via Czechoslovakia, Austria, Italy.

A girl in the death march

After I and all the others standing in line to get a "Security Pass" were arrested by the Hungarian policemen, we started marching toward the Danube. With me was another woman from the marked house. I saw one of the people from the house watching us to see where we were being taken. He stopped beside the Danube. Later I learned that he went back to the house and reported that we had been taken away. I was 13 then, and Mama was very worried.

We were in a brick factory across the Danube one or two nights. From there we started walking about 30 kilometers a day. At night we slept in stables or brick factories. I don't remember any details about our escorts. They were Hungarians, I think Hungarian policemen armed with rifles. They were not violent with us. I was the only girl and I remember them saying: "There's a little girl with us. Why don't you see to it that she's taken from here?" At one point my feet swelled up and I wasn't able to put on my shoes. I said I couldn't go on, but still I walked another 30 kilometers. We stopped at a place called Szony on the Danube. We slept on empty cargo boats. It was awful. I remember us sitting down to rest and a woman sitting down next to me. Afterwards she didn't get up. I saw that she was dead. We walked all day. A Hungarian soldier from our escort took my address and promised to write my family to arrange to get me back.

We arrived at a place called Gonyu and I stopped and said: "Look at my feet. I can't go on. Do whatever you like. I can't walk any more." A Hungarian officer pointed to a certain man and told me to follow him. I remember that that day we were joined by many people from Budapest. I don't know what happened to them, because I joined the man the Hungarian officer had told me to follow. I walked with him till we got to a certain boat, on which he had a cabin. From our conversation I gathered that he was from Austria. He believed that Hitler was going to win the war, but he was willing to help me. He told me that he had a daughter my age and didn't want me to suffer. He took care of everything in that cabin – heating water and poviding food and a place to sleep. We stayed there a few weeks.

One day, we got up very early. He packed some food for me – pork and other things – and we walked to the railroad station. We rode all day on a freight train to Budapest. It was evening when we arrived, and I showed him the way.

Mama was very, very happy to see me, and I thanked the man. I saw him go into a small side room, the servants' room. I guess that in that room they gave him money for bringing me home. I went back to the marked house, and the next day Mama and I had to move into the ghetto.

Husband:	Shraga			
Children:	Sarah	Me'ira	Ruhama	Yom-Tov
Grand-children:	Tal	Aluma	Ze'ev	
	Efrat	Amikam	Ittamar	
	Tamar	Alon	Yosef	
	Ayala	Hodaya	Yishai	
	Ya'ir		Shahar	
	Iddit			

Shraga Shemer (Shirman)

Born 1929 in Hangony, Hungary. Germans come. To Ozd ghetto, May 26, 1944. Conscripted into labor unit, June 6, 1944. To recruitment center at Jolsva end of June. By train to Galicia. Hungarian soldiers' treatment of Jews of labor unit. Some Jews stubbornly observe religious rituals. Retreat through Carpathians toward Hungary, September 1944. Work in factory in Satoraljaujhely. Escape attempt with help of Hungarian soldier. March to Losonc. By freight train to Hagyeshalom; labor there through March 1945. March to Bruck escorted by German soldiers; Jews remaining in Hegyeshalom massacred. Prison in Landesdorf; march to Vienna. Order to massacre Jews just before liberation not carried out. Taken prisoner by Red Army at Sopronlkohida. Jews avoid deportation to Siberia with help of Jewish woman doctor in Red Army. Released by Russians. To Miskolc and Hangony. To Eretz Yisrael via Germany, France and Cyprus, 1947.

66

Sadists for the fun of it

In Galicia we were guarded by the Hungarian army. Our unit commander, a nasty Gentile named Pototzky with a rank equivalent to that of captain in the Israel Defense Forces, was a drunken sadist the likes of whom I have never since seen. He was in the habit of bullying the Jews, except for a few who toadied to him. I twice underwent punishment at his hands. The first: One day I learned that my father was due to arrive where I was. I had not seen Papa for a long time, and of course I missed him. I arranged with a friend to switch jobs: he would go to the place to which I was assigned and I would work at the place where my father was due to come, and in this way I would be able to see him.

A soldier, one of our regular guards, noticed me there and remembered that I was supposed to work at another spot. He asked me what I was doing there and I told him the truth. He was angry, and he took me to Pototzky, who ordered me hung by my hands for two hours. This was one of the severest punishments used in the Hungarian army. The person's hands are tied behind his back with a rope. Another rope is tied to this one and slung around the branch of a tree, and the victim is pulled up and left to hang there. The pain is hellish, indescribable. By Hungarian army orders, two people are assigned to watch the hanging person: an armed soldier and a doctor. Assigned to watch me was the soldier who had reported me to Pototzky and an elderly Jewish doctor who was the doctor of our labor unit. On his sleeve he wore a red, white, and green band, the colors of the Hungarian flag. (Jews who had served with distinction in the Hungarian army in World War I were permitted to wear this band instead of the yellow band Jews in general were required to wear.)

Under the scrutiny of the doctor, when I passed out after an hour they took me down. After they had splashed several buckets of water on me, I came to and they hung me again, for another hour. My father, of blessed memory, arrived after they let me down. It is easy to imagine a father's feelings on seeing his 15-year-old son in such a situation.

As a result of such hanging, one loses control of one's hands. My hands hung limply at my sides as though they were not mine at all, and I was unable to manipulate them. I was not allowed to talk to Papa, and they made me go back to my previous job — carrying slabs of greensward to camouflage the gun positions. I was unable to coordinate my hands, so one of my comrades tied them to each other in such a manner that I was able to lift and carry the slabs. It was quite a few weeks before I regained control of my hands.

The second time Pototzky put me on trial for loading my father's bundle onto the cart during our march. It seems that the Hungarians had mistakenly thought that the bundle was mine, so they tried me again. This time the punishment was "mixed calisthenics," as they called it. This consisted of rolling uphill and jumping and running for two hours; this was especially hard for the older people, but for a youngster like me it was relatively easy.

If not by Pototzky's inspiration, then certainly with his approval, some of the soldiers used to harass not only individual prisoners, but the entire contingent. Often we went out to work escorted by armed Hungarian soldiers. We marched in rows of three abreast, as the army did, the armed soldiers marching on either side of us and bringing up the rear. At the departure points two soldiers with batons planted themselves at each side of the road, and as we marched out they would lay into us with the batons for no reason at all, just for kicks. Sometimes they would also fire their guns into our ranks — for the same reason.

Their sadistic harassment gave them pleasure.

Wife: Rahel

Offspring: Listed with testimony of wife, Rahel Shemer

Eliezer Shimoni (Hauser)

Born 1928 in Feldebro, Hungary. Antisemitism in Nyirbator. Problems because of lack of Hungarian citizenship. News from BBC and refugees from Poland, and Jews' reaction. March from Nyiregyhaza to Auschwitz and selection before entering camp. Attitude to religious precepts in Auschwitz. Death march to Gleiwitz camp, January 17, 1945. Travel in open freight wagons via Czechoslovakia to Buchenwald. Czechs' friendly attitude. Special selection for Jews in Buchenwald, April 1945. Joins transport; last-minute escape. Liberation, May 1945. In uncle's home at Nyirbator. Zionist training camp in Budapest. To Eretz Yisrael, 1946. News of father's fate.

Trapped

From Weimar we travelled to Buchenwald. The Buchenwald main camp branched off into many sub-camps, to which many prisoners were sent. When I arrived in February 1945, there was a tremendous number of prisoners there of various nationalities. I was in the children's camp, far from the entrance gate, behind the adults' camps. My big brother had been with me all the way until we were separated during the journey to Buchenwald. He was about two years older than me, but he was weak, and I had helped him along during all that period. I had given him moral support, and had tried to share with him every day whatever food I was able to get hold of. In Buchenwald we were not put right to work, and I used the time to try to find him. I was overjoyed when I located him in a barrack of older youth.

After about a month I was sent to Holzen camp, a Buchenwald sub-camp not far from Hannover. It was in a marshy area, and conditions there were rough. Every day we had to march several kilometers to work in underground factories in the Hannover area.

With the U.S. Army approaching, we were evacuated to Buchenwald. During the journey back, we saw a lot of German military. Our intuition told us that the war would soon end. But the Germans made the prisoners work right up to the end, as if nothing was happening. As soon as I got back I went looking for my brother and was happy to find him in his barrack. There were thousands of new prisoners in the camp, who had been evacuated there from other camps, and things were becoming chaotic.

On April 4 we suddenly heard an announcement in German over the loudspeakers: "All Jews to the assembly area!" The Jewish prisoners were in a panic and they started rushing about looking for places to hide. The Germans tried to force the Jews to assemble, but to no avail. Then they withheld the regular food rations and promised bread and sausage to those who would go on the transports. The hunt for Jews went on for several days.

I was in block 66 in the children's camp. The block chief was a Czech. He knew what those transports meant, and he did everything he could to save us. Once or twice he couldn't get out of it and our whole barrack had to report to the assembly area. Twice we were saved thanks to the sudden appearance of Allied bombers and the sirens that sent everybody rushing for shelter.

At one point I broke. This was shortly before the liberation. I had lost my brother and didn't know where he was. Apparently he could no longer take the hunger and had gone on one of the transports. I also told myself that I had to eat. I informed them that I was leaving the block and going on a transport.

The transports were arranged in a large hall used as a movie theater. Those caught were placed between two barbed-wire fences leading to the hall's door. I went in, got the food, and instead of going out again with the streaming crowd I did an about-face and went back in. At the far end of the theatre there was a corner that led outside. There was a fence there, and, holding the food, I climbed the fence, threw the food down, and jumped. I hurt myself, but I made my way back to my camp, to block 66. That is how I was saved.

Wife:	Hanna		
Children:	Hayim	Rahel	Giora
Grand-children:	Amihai	Orr	Meital
	Hadar	Noga	Noam
	Michal	Shahar	
	Lior		

69

Hanna Shimoni (nee Gottdiener)

Born 1936 in Debrecen, Hungary. (Named Judith at birth and so called till coming to Eretz Yisrael, when sister registered her as Hanna, which is the name in all her documents.) In Debrecen till German entry. In ghetto, then to brick factory. Train journey to Slovakia, June 1944, and return to Strasshof, Austria. Her family and another one at farm near Heidenreichstein, Austria, July-September 1944. Father dies of illness. Back to Strasshof, then month's work in children's clothing factory, autumn 1944. In Bergen-Belsen, till evacuation in April 1945. At Hilersleben after liberation. Family splits up: children go to Eretz Yisrael and elder members go to Hungary to seek kin. Shimoni with mother in displaced-persons' camp in Belgium, then in uncle's home in France. To Eretz Yisrael as "legal" immigrant, September 1945.

'We shall never separate'

At the end of Passover we were transferred to the Debrecen ghetto. The problems of supporting ourselves had begun before. From the Debrecen period, I especially remember the son of the concierge of the building in which we lived. The building had once been a hotel. Below was a large compound. The concierge's son always scared me. Whenever I wanted to go in, I made sure to do so together with some adult. When things got bad, our family made up that whenever one of us came home, we would whistle a special signal. We lived in an atmosphere of constant suspicion and fear. When the Germans entered Debrecen, they set up their command post in the building opposite, and we hung blankets over the windows, so they shouldn't see what we were doing.

The ghetto was in a strictly Jewish neighborhood. There was a Jewish school. My married sister lived in the the area included in the ghetto. We moved only a few pieces of our furniture. All of us – my parents, my brothers and my sisters – crowded into that tiny apartment and we slept two to a bed.

I remember a heavy air raid when we went down to the shelters. When the bombing was over the people went out to clear the rubble and attend to the wounded. My brothers also went out. When they came back, they said the balcony of our building had collapsed. Later we learned that the whole building had been destroyed.

We had taken along to the ghetto all the flour and oil in our pantry. Mama and my sisters constantly baked cookies and other things. I remember them putting jewelry into the cookies, and coloring Papa's gold cufflinks black to camouflage them.

We were in the ghetto a few weeks. In June 1944 they rounded us up, piled us into trucks and moved us to the brick factory. The place was packed; they seem to have brought all the Jews of the region there. We were moved from place to place with our bundles, and around us marched gendarmes bearing whips.

My big sister was very pretty. She seems to have attracted the attention of one of the gendarmes – a young fellow of about 18. He hit her across the back with his whip. My sister picked up a wooden tub and was about to throw it at his head, but my two brothers grabbed her and stopped her. If she had done what she intended, she would have been killed on the spot.

I also had a difficult experience at this time. I had long braids and didn't want my hair cut. One day I heard my named being called. There was a big crowd there and I was frightened. Mama said: "Go! Go!" She apparently knew why I was being called. I went, and they shaved my skull clean. Mama was unhappy. She had been worried about our hygiene, but she hadn't expected such an outcome. For me it was a trauma, the first trauma of my life. I was eight at the time.

I remember how the big families were separated from the small ones. Papa and Mama held a consultation with my big brothers about whether it might not be a good idea to split up the family. Small families might have a better chance of survival. It was decided that come what may, we will never split up! So we joined the group of large families.

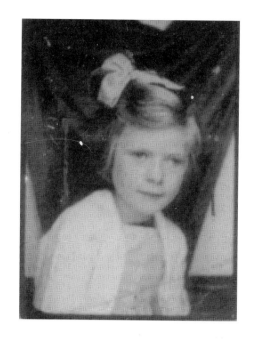

Husband: Eliezer

Offspring: Listed with testimony of husband, Eliezer Shimoni

71

Sarah Singer (nee Najol)

Born 1927 in Teglas, Hungary. Life there and in Hajduhadhaz. Work under German supervision in textile factory in Debrecen. Debrecen ghetto, August 1943. Ghetto inhabitants sent by train toward Czech border, June 1944, and back to Austria. Strasshof camp. Gutweisend farm, July through December. Short stay in Strasshof. Teresienstadt from shortly before liberation till June 1945. Bnai Akiva religious Zionist youth training camps in Hungary. To Israel, June 1948.

The gentlemen

Before the Germans arrived, the economic situation had got progressively worse. Bread coupons were issued, and we bakers had to paste the coupons on sheets every month and take the sheets to the Town Hall, where they were checked to see if we had stolen anything. The weight of the bread never jibed with the record. The bread was supposed to weigh 40 per cent more than the flour, and the account was supposed to jibe with that. But it came to less, because the flour weighed less than what was recorded. A fine was imposed each time, and we had to buy flour on the black market to make up the difference. In the end we, the bakers, went starving for a piece of bread. They treated the Gentiles the same way...

In the Town Hall a clerk who had been a classmate of mine had to check my accounts. She asked me to help her, because she was unable to manage all the arithmetic. Each month I would come with my papers, take a seat, and add up the month's figures.

One day some time after the Germans had occupied Hungary, I had to take my accounts to the Town Hall. Shortly before that we had been told to prepare the yellow patch we were to wear. Fortunately, we had been told to put it on the front of our garment and not on the back. When I arrived at the office, there were no Germans there. When I left, the stairs – they were wide stairs – were all filled from top to bottom with Germans, I didn't know what to do. I covered the patch with my folder full of papers. I thought: What now? How will I get down? How will I pass between them? They were all over the place, a mass of them, at least hundreds of German soldiers. And the stairs...

I pretended that I hadn't noticed anything special happening. I went out and started walking: what will be will be. What else can I do? When the officer saw me, he ordered the soldiers to move to the sides of the staircase, clearing the center, and to stand at attention. I thought I would pass out on the spot. They stood at attention, and the officer courteously gestured with his hand for me to pass. I went down the stairs barely restraining a smile. Nothing happened. When I turned the corner and knew I was no longer in their sight, I went into a mad dash home, charged into my house and fainted. To this day I don't understand what happened. But that sort of thing also happened.

Husband:	Shlomo			
Children:	Nehama	Nurit	Daliah	Rafael
Grand-children:	Iddo	Yehuda	Yael	Tehilla
	Hilli	Shirri	Michal	Tamar
	Littal	Noa	Yarden	Semadar
				Naftali
				Adi
				Hadas
				Ovadiah

Rahel Snir-Schindler (nee Goldstein)

Born 1930 in Nyirvaja village, attached to Nyirmada town, Hungary. Parents' home: education, occupation, Jewish and non-Jewish lifestyles, relations between Jews and Gentiles, customs. Situation of Jews and relations with Christians before and after 1943. Germans arrive. Six weeks in Kisvarda ghetto. All eight members of family deported to Auschwitz. Selection, Camp C, block 32. To Stutthof six weeks later. Work on farm near Stutthof. Back to Stutthof camp. Torn. Work on dugouts three weeks, then back to Stutthof. Magdeburg weapons factory. Relations between women prisoners. Flight of SS men from Magdeburg and their return. March to Elbe River under heavy bombardment on way to Altengrabow. Liberated by Russians. Frankfurt, Berlin and home. To Israel, 1949.

Ties and impediments

I went to a Hungarian school in the village together with Gentile children from the village and nearby farms. For the first and second grades I attended the Catholic school. Then I went to the Protestant school, which was bigger and on a higher level. The atmosphere there was more antisemitic. The school was dominated by a family of teachers named Vitzner.

I remember how in 1940 they took up a collection at school to buy flags for their brothers in the Hungarian Army and the teacher announced: "Jews don't have to bring money. We won't use Jewish money to buy flags for our brothers." We reported this at home. There was a Jewish officer home on leave at the time. He went and told the teacher: "If you have no need of our money, why should I serve?" This caused a furor, and the teacher apologized.

Always on our way home from school, a band of Christian children waited for us Jewish children at the bridge, with sticks, and they would beat us, shouting: "Stinking Jews, go to Palestine!" My brother, a feisty boy, would hit back.

Till 1941-1942 we were friendly with our neighbor's daughters and would visit them at home. Their father would offer us pork. We brought him newspapers we got from Budapest, and at Passover time we gave them matzot. They would bring us the lessons we missed by not attending school on the Sabbath. As time went by, we cut off our contact with them. Our parents thought we should stop associating with Gentiles: they practiced free love; girls got pregnant and had abortions; a local Gentile doctor made his living just performing abortions. I remember our neighbor's daughter, my friend Ilus, telling me that her sister, Ilma, had jumped down from the attic, because she was pregnant and wanted to get rid of the baby that way. In the village there were also fathers who raped their daughters. The Jewish girls were protected.

There was a family of aristocrats in the village whose property was managed by a work foreman. He didn't like Jews, but we got along well with him, and it might even be said that Papa was "his Jew."

In 1941, when Papa's work permit was taken from him, this man offered to employ me and my sister in his apple orchard. He paid us as he did his other workers.

When we went into the ghetto, he drove up there in a carriage and offered to protect my two older sisters by taking them on as "Hungarian" workers in one of the homes he managed some distance from the village. Mama wouldn't agree, saying: "How can I let my daughters eat non-kosher food?"

When we came back after the liberation, he wouldn't re-establish contact with us. He was apparently afraid of the neighbors, who had labelled him a "Jew-lover."

Husband:	Shevah		
Children:	Avraham*	Dina	Yossi
Grand-children:		Moriah	Avraham
		Rama	Revital
		Golan	Oron
		Omer	Ittai

* of blessed memory

75

Eliahu Sprei

Born 1923 in Mezocsat, Hungary. Life in Mezocsat. Ideals of Jewish culture in Hungarian milieu. Informed upon, tried on charges of speculation. Sister's trouble obtaining Hungarian citizenship because of stay and marriage in Czechoslovakia. News from Czechoslovakia. Hiding cousins from Czechoslovakia. He and brother in forced-labor units in Jolsva region and Ujhely. Hungarian commander. Hides in home of Ujhely Police master-sergeant for week till liberated by Russians. Russian soldiers rape all Hungarian women in Mezocsat. Return to Mezocsat. Owning farm, agricultural research, activity at Bnai Akiva religious Zionist youth training camp till move to Israel in 1949.

'Sprei knows'

From Jolseva we went in the direction of the eastern Carpathians. Our unit was supposed to deliver ammunition to the front and bring back the wounded and the dead.

The commander was a professional antisemite. He had studied to be a priest. He said he had been to Palestine three times. He owned a large estate, and was an adventurer. What can I say? He always had to have Jews around him. We had no idea why, but that was the fact. My brother, for example – without my brother that fellow wouldn't budge.

Once cash had to be brought from Budapest. He sent his deputy – a quiet, liberal Gentile, Kecslen – and my brother, who was his "personal assistant." Since he was unable to be without a Jew, he took my other brother, who cooked for the Jews. (The chief cook worked for the officers.) He engaged him, too, in philosophical and theological discussions. Once he told him: "You're all right, too, only not as good as your brother the Chief Rabbi." But when something didn't please him, he became murderous. He didn't literally murder, but people sometimes died as a result of being hung by their hands over their heads at his order. He drank a lot and liked women, and he would come back black and blue. The chief cook was a cynical Gentile, a house painter by trade. He introduced himself to us by saying: "I'm like Hitler." He was unable to reconcile himself to the fact that a Jew was a cook, and especially to the fact that we three brothers always had jobs. We did not get these jobs as a result of favoritism, but because there were tasks that needed to be performed. For example, straps were always tearing, and when they asked who knew how to repair them I would volunteer. I had not yet finished the job when the commander asked for someone to polish his shoes. When he would ask why his shoes weren't sparkling, my brother said:

"Because I don't have a brush. But my brother knows how to do it." And do it I did: I took hair from a stallion's tail, not from a mare's, and a piece of board and built a brush. He was pleased, so pleased that he spread the word everywhere: Sprei knows how to do everything.

Wife: Bella

Esther Steinmetz (nee Feldheim)

Born 1926 in Foldes, Hungary. Germans come, Passover 1944. Banished to Puspokladany, then to Debrecen. Work in brick factory. Deported to Auschwitz, Camp II, block 8. To Ravensbrueck, then Berlin-Schoenholz-Reinickendorf. Work in factory making airplane spare parts. To Sachsenhausen and onward in three-week march. Liberated by Russians not far from Stuttgart. Visit to Foldes, training camp, "illegal" immigration to Eretz Yisrael (half year in Cyprus detention).

We didn't know what they had in mind

From Puspokladany we were moved to Debrecen. We were concentrated in a place that had been a tannery. One day a week later, all families with a large number of adults were ordered to line up outside. Nobody knew what they were up to. I was with my parents and my sister and her 11-year-old daughter. Except for my niece, we were all adults. My father was sure they meant to deport us and said he had no intention of going outside, for who knew?... Long afterwards we heard they had been sent to Austria to work. The next day we were taken to Auschwitz. Many people had joined their families and gone to Austria. Only sick people had remained.

The next day we were taken with the large families to Auschwitz. We set out from Debrecen in June 1944. I don't remember how long the trip took, but it was quite long. They put us in cattle cars – women, old people and children – about 70-75 people to a car. Many died en route. We weren't familiar with the route, and we had no idea where they were taking us. Sometimes we managed to peek out between the slats, but we had no idea where we were or why we were there. We didn't have an inkling, till we arrived.

On our arrival, the Jews working there opened the wagon doors and told us to hurry down and leave our bundles there. They spoke Yiddish. Some of them managed to get close to us and tell us to hand the children to the older parents. Many refused, and my sister said she would not hand over her daughter. The men were taken away immediately. That's how we were immediately separated from Papa. I, my mother and my sister and her daughter went as a group. Mengele conducted the selection. When I passed by with my mother and sister, he signalled with his hand for me to approach him. He asked me in German how old I was and I told him. He grabbed me and shoved me to the right. The young people from my village had already moved on ahead, and I managed to hear my mother's shout from behind me: "Hurry, catch up, don't remain alone!" Those were the last words I ever heard from her. I never saw her again – not her nor any other member of my family.

We were immediately taken to be disinfected and to wash up. They took my clothing and shoes, and gave me a pair of Dutch-style wooden clogs. It was hard for me to walk in them. We arrived at the camp. We still had no idea what was happening. Some said it was only a temporary separation, and we would see our parents again in a few days. We didn't recognize each other, because they had shaved our heads. We looked at each other and asked each other when we would again see our parents, our brothers, our sisters. When they heard us, they shouted: "See that smoke there? That's where your parents are!" Only then it began to dawn on us what was happening.

Husband:	Yaacov		
Children:	Menahem	Amnon	Moshe
Grand-children:	Oshrat	Perah	Renana
	Rafael	Sarah	Moriah
		Bat-Chen	

Yaacov Steinmetz

Born 1926 in Mezokovesd, Hungary. Parents' home. Drafted into labor unit. To Jolsva on Czech-Hungarian border. Labor at Hejocsaba near Miskolc. Labor at Putnok. Tending and guarding horses of Hungarian Army. In hospital at Szerencs. Budapest – labor under German supervision. Liberated by Russians. Return to Mezokovesd. Zionist training camp in Hungary. To Israel via Austria and Italy, 1948.

Not the sort of liberation we expected

One morning in January we woke up to discover that the Germans were gone. At night we had still heard sporadic gunfire, but when we looked out the window in the morning, we realized that no Germans were around.

The liberation was not as we had imagined it. The Russians sent many Jews to labor camps in the Soviet Union, where some of them met their death.

I and my brother-in-law waited a few days before we went out of the ghetto. We had decided that it wasn't worth taking risks, and that having suffered so long, we could endure another few days. After a while we decided to go out. We started walking. After we had walked a stretch, a group of Russian soldiers stopped us. I showed them my yellow patch, and we told them that we were Jews and that we had suffered a long time under Hungarian and German rule. I asked them to let us continue on. They said that it made no difference that we were Jews, and that whether we were Jews or Germans, we would have to work. There was an officer in that group – a Jew, I assume – who took us aside and advised us to run for it and not to show our faces in the area again.

It was late at night and we had no idea where to go. We knocked at a Hungarian Gentile's door and asked him to let us in. He welcomed us and even offered us a bed. We were crawling with lice, and we did the decent thing and declined his offer. He didn't understand why. In the morning we ate in his home. He advised us to wait, so we shouldn't be caught by the Russians again. We didn't listen to him. We went out, and again we were caught – by a Russian soldier. Again we explained that we were Jews and had suffered a great deal during the war. It was no use. We were taken to a certain place in Budapest, where they gave us a saw and put us to work. We realized that we shouldn't stay there, and we succeeded in fleeing to the railroad station and got on a train. After travelling a few kilometres, Russian soldiers came aboard and wanted to conscript us for labor. We left our bundles on the train and succeeded in slipping away.

And so, after many obstacles and delays, I returned to Mezokovesd, my birthplace. There we found Jews – broken wretches, mainly survivors of the forced-labor units. From those Jews I learned that my brother had arrived and was in a nearby village. I sent him a message and we met a few days later. We waited patiently for our parents, until a certain Jew, a survivor of the camps, arrived and told us we had nothing to wait for. This was the first time we heard about Auschwitz. He told us we would never see our parents again: they had been burnt in the crematorium. That was the first time I heard of a crematorium. Even then we didn't believe it, and we kept hoping that maybe someone of the family had survived. Unfortunately, it was a vain hope. We had been a big family – six sisters and four brothers. Out of that conflagration only the two of us remained – my brother and I.

I stayed in Mezokovesd a few months, and we realized that there was no point remaining there. At this stage some young people started organizing *hachsharot*, Zionist training camps. Before that, I had never heard of a *hachshara*. Our community had been a very pious one, which did not tolerate Zionist activity. I joined a *hachshara* of the Bnai Akiva religious Zionist youth movement, and in 1947 a group of us left Hungary with the intention of entering Eretz Yisrael in the framework of the "illegal immigration." After a while we sailed from an Italian port. Destination: Eretz Yisrael.

Wife: Esther

Offspring: Listed with testimony of wife, Esther Steinmetz

81

Hayim Taub

Born 1929 in Nyiregyhaza, Hungary. Jews' attitude to Hungary and Zionism. Transfer to ghetto, spring 1944. Two weeks at Harangos farm. Auschwitz. Labor camp at Dyhernfurth. Father rescues him. Funfteichen camp. Wustegiersdorf camp. Dornau camp. Germans present him to Red Cross delegation as model, January 1945. Schotenburg camp. Liberated by Russians, May 1945. Return to Hungary. Inner struggle over faith. Bnai Akiva training camp. To Israel, 1948.

Rescued from the 'rest home'

We arrived at Dyhernfurth from Auschwitz. They assigned us to special work in a plant producing all sorts of things. I was assigned to the soldering section. There was a huge metals workshop where pipes had to be cleaned with sand. I and a friend were given this job. With great difficulty, and wearing a mask, I crawled in to clean those six-meter-long pipes. We went in, and did not come out till we had finished. I felt that if I went on working there another week or two, I would collapse. I remember telling the Ukrainian *kapo* that I would not go on, no matter what. He called the SS man. I said I couldn't go on working that way: they should either reduce my hours or assign me to another job. I remember opening my shirt and saying, in Yiddish: "You can kill me if you want." I thought the SS man understood me, but he asked the Ukrainian: "What'd he say?" The Ukrainian answered in German: "You can kill him." The SS man was a young fellow, and I couldn't have picked him out in a crowd of a hundred people. But I remember him saying: "Get back to work." Of course, the *kapo* hit me, and I went on working there.

I had another solution: I deliberately stepped on a rusty nail and got my foot infected. There was a hospital in the camp, and I thought they would put me there, and then, after a while, assign me to another job. My foot really swelled up and I was hospitalized. There they were drawing up a list of people who wanted to go to a rest home, at Gross-Rosen. I didn't know exactly what Gross-Rosen was, so I signed up. From my hospital window I called down to my father, of blessed memory, that I had signed up for Gross-Rosen. He shouted: "What have you done?! Why did you do that?!" All I know is that when the group left for Gross-Rosen, I wasn't in it. Later, when I left the hospital, I learned that

Papa and my uncle had got me off the list. I don't know how; maybe they bribed the doctors or the people who drew up the list.

As far as I know, people who went to the Gross-Rosen "rest home" haven't returned to this day. Us they had told: a week's rest at the home, to get better so as to be able to go back to work. How was it supposed to occur to me that it wasn't a rest home? That it was the notorious crematorium?

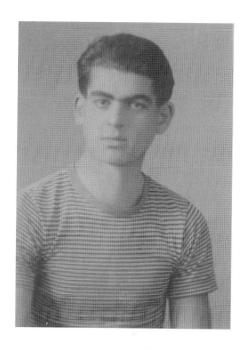

Wife:	Yona		
Children:	Ofra	Ze'ev	Sarah
Grand-children:	Erez	Inbal	Roni
	Barak	Raanan	Raz
	Gur	Alon	Nitzan
	David	Kfir	
	Hilla		

83

Yona Taub (nee Ortsmann)

Born 1931 in Berlin. Family, in Brussels, flees to southern France when Germans invade Belgium, May 1940. Toulouse. Nice. Parents help smuggle Jews from Belgium to southern France. Father arrested, sent to Drancy camp, August 1942. Father reportedly in Mechtal camp in Germany, October 1942-September 1943. With mother in Nice till Germans enter Italian zone. Mother, disguised as Christian, in home of Christians in village. Failed attempt to move Taub and other children to Switzerland. Return to Grenoble. Steal across Swiss border. With Christian family in Switzerland. Returns to Belgium, rejoins mother. Bnai Akiva training camp. Eretz Yisrael, June 1946.

'I want my Mama'

In September 1943 the Germans entered Nice and the situation of the Jews there worsened. There was an organization, O.S.E. (Oeuvre de Secour aux Enfants) that arranged for children to be transferred to Switzerland. Only children and the elderly were sent. The Swiss turned back everyone between ages 15 or 16 and 60. When these were captured by the Germans, they were sent to Auschwitz. We – three children from Nice – were sent with a group of children by rail to Grenoble near the Swiss border. One day it was decided that during the night we would steal across the border to Switzerland. There were 13 of us - a mother and her baby, an elderly couple and, I think, 10 children. That night we were driven to the border area and we started walking through the woods with the man who smuggled people across the border. Suddenly a German patrol with huge hounds appeared. Our guide told us to scatter: "Try to save yourselves; there's nothing more I can do for you."

The patrol got wind of us. I ran and ran. I climbed a tree. The mother also ran with her baby. As she fled, she dropped her sack under a tree. Everything fell out and the contents of a bottle of perfume spilled. The Germans, helped by their hounds, caught the whole group. Only I wasn't caught. The fragrance of the perfume had apparently confused the dogs. I spent some miserable hours up in the tree till midnight.

At midnight, someone appeared and called to me: "Little girl, little girl, come down, I'll help you." It was one of the forest wardens, perhaps a member of the French Underground. He took me to the village and hid me in a barn. He told me to be very careful, as the Germans were in the area, conducting checks every night. In fact, they did come and they poked around inside the haystacks with pitchforks. Luckily, they passed me by without noticing me. The next day I was sent back to Grenoble.

I was a girl of 12 and didn't know a soul. Somehow I remembered the office where we had once registered and I made my way back there. It was on the main street, and SS men were stationed there. I didn't know what to do. A woman stood there looking at me. She warned me not to enter the building and took me home with her.

When I got to the house – I'll never forget this – I said: "I want to go home to my Mama! What am I doing here? I don't want anything, I just want my Mama! I'm writing my Mama everything right now and we'll send it to the Gentile lady in whose house she's living." But they said: "No, you're not going home. We'll arrange to get you to the border again."

Three days later I set out once more to steal across the border into Switzerland. This time it succeeded.

Husband: Hayim

Offspring: Listed with testimony of husband, Hayim Taub

Esther (Magdi) Unger (nee Fried)

Born 1928 in Sarret Udvari, Hungary. Effects of antisemitic policy on Jewish life from 1938. Extremist-antisemitic Nyilasok gangs attack Jews. Corresponds with cousin in Hungarian labor unit, May 1944. Nagyvarad ghetto. Auschwitz - Birkenau, Ravensbrveik, Berlin- Scheinolz, Reinickendorf camp till April 1945. Death march to Sachsenhausen and Freienstadt till liberation. Attitude of Russians. To Budapest via Dresden and Prague. Father's fate. Bnai Akiva training camp in Hungary till move to Israel, June 1948.

Between trepidation and hope

Our family's daily life fluctuated between trepidation and hope. My parents read in the newspapers about the situation on the Russian front and about the Russian Army's rapid advance. They thought this might be our salvation. In fact, that wasn't far from the truth.

We stayed in the house and spoke a great deal about the situation of the Jews. At long last I squeezed a promise out of my father that when the war was over we wouldn't go on living in Hungary – we would go to Eretz Yisrael.

I was 16. The previous winter, a close relationship had developed between me and my cousin Erno Berkovits. So it was only natural that we should write to each other when he was taken to the forced-labor camp. I managed to save one of his letters to me...

Let's go back to Papa's fate and how our correspondence was found. My father was taken to a forced-labor camp four days before we were taken to the Nagyvarad ghetto. We got to say goodbye to each other at the railroad station. My father was released from the Hungarian forced-labor camp in September 1944 and died on Shevat 12, 5705-January 26, 1945 from a beating by the Russian "liberators."

When the war ended, I went back to my native village. My heart pounded as I entered our house... I had no illusions... All I could hear was the voices of my dear ones echoing in that desolation... Papa had managed to fix up the house a bit for the surviving family members... Even my sewing-machine was among the items my father retrieved from the Gentile homes, and I managed to bring it along to Israel; I still have it.

...I roamed from room to room... In one room there was a solitary couch, on which my father, of blessed memory, had spent his nights... I remembered dear

Papa, whom our whole family had loved so...and in the end had died alone, with no one at his bedside. Incidentally, he received the postcard I sent from Auschwitz care of neighbors.

There were feathers all over my room. Hostile hands must have looked for valuables... I groped amid the feathers and found an envelope - containing the letter of my cousin Erno and also the letter I had sent him.

At that time I didn't fully appreciate the value of those letters. I have kept them as living mementoes of those times:

"Dear Magda! In your letter you write that you never thought that this is what life would be like. I can say the same. Life has its disappointments. Life's disappointments – or so we at least hope – turn into pleasanter things. All we can do is believe and hope that everything will turn out all right. We mustn't lose 'Hope' – "Tikva" – [the name of the Zionist hymn, today the Israeli national anthem]."

And my letter:

"Dear Erno! Your letter found us at home, thank God. I can't tell you how delighted we are when evening comes, giving us a chance to relax a bit. You probably also want to hear some good news, not just bad news, but I have no words of comfort at all to write you. 'Let's have no illusions,' you write in your last letter. But that's all we have left. At such a time we at least forget a little. The thought of leaving for the ghetto is with us constantly. I can't decide which of my effects to take along. The thought that we'll have to leave everything behind is a painful one. You wrote that the torrent swept you along. Now it has swept us, too. The question is: will we stay afloat, or will we sink? God only knows. But we go on hoping – the only thing keeping us alive is hope."

Husband:	Yaacov			
Children:	Nitzhiya	Naomi	Ronit	Naftali
Grand-children:	Shira	Taffat	Maayan	
	Noam	Daniel	Yiftah	
		Elyashiv		
		Gilboa		
		Nofar		

87

Naftali Weinberger

Born 1928 in Szarvas, Hungary. Jewish communal life before German arrival. From Szarvas ghetto to Szolnok, April 1944. By train to Strasshof camp, Austria. Labor at Potendorf farm till November 1944. Back to Strasshof and deported to Bergen-Belsen, end November. In Bergen-Belsen, evacuation and march to railroad station. Liberated by Americans. In Farsleben and Millersleben after liberation.

For Papa

In April they started evacuating the people from the Bergen-Belsen camp. The first transport was of Hungarian and Dutch Jews from the *Sonderlager*. Each of us was given bread and a can of preserves. We started marching to the railway station 6-7 kilometers away. My father was very feeble. His face was swollen. He had diarrhea and was barely able to walk. Mama and my sisters carried their own bundles while I carried mine and Papa's. We had marched about 3-4 kilometers when I realized it was getting dark, and I rushed ahead to the head of the procession. On reaching the train, I and several acquaintances seized places in one of the wagons and I rushed back to help Papa. I knew what was likely to happen to anyone left behind. The road was a difficult one, climbing and descending sharply. On either side was the German army. Among the soldiers were many *Volksdeutsche*, ethnic Germans, many of them from Hungary, who hurled threats and curses at us as we passed. When I got to the top of a hill, an SS man, one of those escorting our procession, who spoke fluent Hungarian and was apparently a *Volksdeutscher*, stopped me and asked: "Is that your father sitting on that rock up there?" I saw Papa sitting on a rock. Apparently, he was unable to go on. The soldier said he would wait till I got him. "If you don't bring him," he said, "the soldiers will kill him." I, a 16-year-old boy, ran madly. Papa hugged me and said: "I thought I'd never see you again." He was totally spent. I carried him on my shoulders till we got to that soldier. We walked together to try to catch up to the rear of the procession. Along the way the soldiers from the camps threatened us, and the SS soldier threatened them back, waving his gun at them and shouting: "Go be heroes at the front, not here against unarmed people!" Gradually, with our last strength, we reached the train.

We were liberated by the Americans. My father was very weak and was sent to the hospital and Farsleben. We were sent to Millersleben. We lived in villas that had been occupied by SS people. When I visited the hospital, I couldn't find my father. He had died a week after the liberation, on the 8th of [the Jewish month] Iyar. He had been buried in a mass grave in a corner of the Farsleben cemetery. The man in charge of the cemetery told me that a number of people had been buried together that day, and there was no way of knowing where Papa was buried. Before I left I asked the chairman of the Magdeburg Jewish community to see to it that the cemetery was tended, that a fence was built around it, and that a monument to the victims was put up.

Two days after the liberation I met that SS soldier, dressed in civilian clothes. He said he wanted to go home to his family, and he had no time to go to a prisoner-of-war camp. He asked me not to tell anyone about him. I promised: "I won't say a word. But if someone else informs on you..." I don't know if anyone did. I never set eyes on him again. I only want to say that I couldn't have informed on him. In any event they were released a few months later.

Wife:	Rahel			
Children:	Malka	Esther	Zvia	Mordechai
Grand-children:	Amihud	Avraham	Netanel	
	Esther	Ro'i	Ittamar	
		Keren	Renana	

89

David Weiss

Born 1923 in Mako, Hungary. Mako Hungarians' antisemitism. Discrimination against Jews in Levente, Hungarian pre-army youth formation. Attitude to Jews in forced-labor units in Don region till and during Russian offensive, December 1942-January 1943, and brother's death (according to reports). Drafted into forced-labor unit in February 1943. Released for a while. Redrafted, February 1944. Labor in Carpathians and Galicia. Prisoner of Russians, summer 1944-1948, in prisoner-of-war camps at Starij-Sambor and Novie-Sambor and near Barvenkovo in Ukrain. In Briansk forests on work assignment from commandant. How Israel's Proclamation of Independence affects treatment of Jews in prisoner-of-war camp near Kharkov. News of fate of parents, who were in group of 99 Jews murdered by Germans in Austria at time of liberation. To Eretz Yisrael, 1948.

90

I and the commandant

It happened in 1946. I had been in Russia two years already, near the city of Barvenkovo. I was in a hospital for prisoners-of-war, together with German and Hungarian prisoners-of-war. I had just recovered from a bout of malaria, and had begun to work in the carpentry shop along with two Jewish comrades.

We were 24 Jews out of several thousand prisoners of various nationalities in the camp. The camp's deputy commandant used to visit the carpentry shop. I don't know why he picked me, but he asked me whether I could undertake an independent assignment, for the purpose of which he would assign eight German prisoners-of-war to me. The truth is that I was suspicious; I was afraid of him, because he did not care for Jews.

In the end I agreed. The assignment was to build him a stable for horses and a barn for cows and other animals. Since there was no material to build the stable, I was to travel 160 kilometers to the famous Briansk forest in Russia. And so, one morning we harnessed horses to the sleds – four horses to a sled – and set out: I, eight German prisoners-of-war and the Russian soldier escorting us. It was snowing and we rode through open country, with nothing to shield us against the biting frost. Thus we travelled till nightfall. The snowfall thickened. Suddenly a pack of howling wolves emerged out of the darkness. They approached us. We could clearly make them out by the light of the moon. We were terrified, but the Russian soldier reassured us, and every time they approached he would fire at them till they ran off. At those moments I recalled what my father, of blessed memory, had told us of his experiences in World War I in Russia. At last we arrived at the edge of the forest. Fortunately, we immediately found a solitary house, which, so it appeared, had belonged to the town sentries.

After a short rest we started chopping down trees. We were at it for nearly six months, till one day the deputy camp commandant appeared and told us to load the trees and return to camp.

As soon as we got back I went to work building the stable. I oversaw the Germans, who worked according to my instructions. This gave me a good feeling, for there I was, a Jew who had survived the Holocaust, after all the suffering I had endured because of the Germans – I, of all people, was in charge of them and they had to take orders from me. There was no vengeance in it, but it certainly felt good.

Moreover, I was pleased that the deputy commandant completely relied on me and did so openly. When the stable was finished, he told me that he had not believed that I, a Jew, would do such a good job.

He invited me to lunch at his home, and we chatted while we ate. I told him and his wife what my family had undergone in the Holocaust, and at the end I could see tears running from his and his wife's eyes. We parted friends, with him showering praises on me.

Wife:	Haya	
Children:	Yaffa	Shabtai
Grand-children:	Odelia	Liat
	Sivan	
	Liron	

Yisrael Weiss

Born 1926 in Tiszakeszi, Hungary. Schooling in village and nearby Mezocsat, and in yeshivot at Tasnad (Transylvania) and Salgotarjan (Hungary). Father and brother drafted into punishment platoon in Ukraine, 1942-43. Entire family in Mezocsat ghetto. Putnok labor camp. Brother to Jolsva labor camp. Kummadaras labor camp at air field several months. Hatvan: clearing rubble after air raids. To Budapest with *Schutzpass*. To Bruck camp, Austria, by train. March from Bruck to Danube. By boat to Mauthausen. Death march to Gunskirchen. Liberation by Americans at Gunskirchen, May 4, 1945. Hospital at Wels. Dornach camp. March east under Russian guard. Escape to Budapest via Vienna. Return to Tiszakeszi. Budapest. Zionist training camp. To Eretz Yisrael via Austria and Italy.

The murderer wears himself out

From Budapest we went by train to Hegyeshalom on the Austro-Hungarian border. We continued on to the Bruck camp in Austria. There they put us into barns of a sort. Each of us was assigned to a straw mattress, and every morning we went to work. Conditions were worse than they had been in Hungary. We were poorly fed, though the work was very hard. I was especially bothered by the fierce cold. The SS staff were an extremely cruel bunch. There were beatings and torture, and people died every day.

I remember one day in particular. That day Allied aircraft bombed the area. The staff were terrified of the air raids, and whenever the alarm sounded they ran off to the shelter, leaving us unguarded. We got a break of half an hour or so, for they never collected us before the all-clear sounded. I and two comrades exploited one of the air-raid alarms to rush off to a nearby farm to get food. The three of us walked to the village, where there was animal fodder: sugar beet and the wastes from the sugar production. We returned immediately, assuming we would be back before the all-clear sounded and the SS men returned.

On our way back, we could see in the distance that a rollcall lineup was in progress. It was being conducted by the cruellest member of the SS staff. He was nicknamed "Gunar", Hungarian for goose, because of his height and long neck. There was no escape for us. He asked where we had been and what we had done, and ordered the Jewish foreman of our work team to give us a beating. The man did his best, but that did not satisfy Gunar. He took the club and laid into us. I didn't think we would get out of that alive. We were battered and bruised all over, but we had to go back to work.

We were working in a deep anti-tank ditch. As a further punishment, I had to carry buckets of mud out of the ditch up a steep, smooth, wet slope. And when, after tremendous effort, with the help of my fingernails, I finally made it to the top, I was shoved back down again and again until I was unable to go on.

We moved to another spot. My yellow patch was not exactly where it was supposed to be, and again I was given a murderous beating. I was all covered with blood and mud, and my clothes were in tatters. Some local Austrian women passed by, and when they saw me they shook their heads, and I could see their shocked looks.

When I got back to camp Gunar was there again, with a single purpose: to beat us. This time he showed up with a German we didn't recognize, and asked: "Where are the three who ran away?" I thought: This is the end. The German spoke no language but German. He asked if any of us knew German. I did – not fluently, but I could understand and answer in the language. I didn't say anything. The eldest of the three of us said he knew German. He must have been just over 40 years old, and I was barely 19. The German asked him: "Don't you know it's forbidden to run away during an air raid?" What could the man reply? The German laid into him with all his might. A few days later the man died from the beating, from nothing else. Then the German went over to the second man, who was also older than me, and also laid into him till he had got his sadistic satisfaction. Then he came over to me, Number 3, and said: "Don't you know that it's forbidden to run away?" I replied: "I saw people older than me going, so I went along." I didn't get so many blows – because he believed me, or maybe he was worn out.

Wife:	Tova		
Children:	Yeshayahu	Esther	Miriam
Grand-children:	Mattan	Naama	Gal
	Nirit	Michal	
	Yaacov	Avinoam	
	Yishai	Ivri	
		Avihai	

David Wilheim

Born 1928 in Vac, Hungary. Forced labor in German headquarters in Budapest, then in mobile German headquarters near Gyor. Work on defense line in Sachendorf camp, Austria. Death march to Mauthausen then to Gunskirchen. From Wels camp to Hungary. To Eretz Yisrael as "illegal immigrant" with Bnai Akiva religious Zionist youth group.

'Games' they played

From the Gyor ghetto we walked to the Sachendorf camp in Austria, near the Hungarian border. The camp was really a complex of three camps. I was in the second one. We lived in a hayloft and we worked at digging anti-tank ditches along a line of hundreds of kilometers. It was March. We didn't get enough to eat and we were famished. The Germans told the sick people to report to hospital. They were taken away from there. It was reported that they were then shot and buried. A few days later we all knew that we mustn't get sick.

One Sunday afternoon, when we weren't working, a fellow of about 20 came to me and suggested that we steal potatoes from a nearby farm. We took sacks and filled them with potatoes. When we returned we saw the German sentry, a boy of about 16 or 17, a member of the Hitler Jugend. He was carrying a rifle and he didn't speak a good Hungarian. He stopped us and said: "I've caught you! Stand up against the wall, both of you!" We did so, and he opened his rifle, took out a bullet and said: "See this bullet? Now you're getting it in the head!" He turned around, while we... He loaded the bullet in the rifle, again took it out, and again said: "Now you're getting a bullet in the head." This went on for about five minutes, but to me it seemed an eternity. Then he sent us to a Jew who was in charge of the camp. He shouted at us for having taken potatoes. He slapped my comrade and whipped me with his belt, telling us that tomorrow we would both be tied to the gallows. Then he ordered us to take the potatoes and go. Each of us had five kilograms of potatoes, which was a big thing.

On the eve of Passover we heard gunfire and we knew that the Russian army was approaching. An order came that everybody able to walk should get ready. We wanted to stay. One of our buddies reported that two Jews had fled and reached a camp in Hungary. The Germans said that those who could walk should walk, and those who wanted to ride should get into the bus. All those unable to go would be left behind. Some people got on the bus. Later, two Jews who managed to escape came and told us that at night they were taken to an unknown place, where the Jews were slaughtered. The pits had been ready in advance. About half the people stayed in the camp. We had decided to walk. An SS officer was also left behind, and we were sure that none of the Jews would be left alive. A few days after we set out on the march that officer showed up and reported that everybody who had remained in the camp was dead, killed in a Russian bombardment.

After the liberation I went to Budapest. I met a Jew who had been with us in Sachendorf, and we chatted. I thought that all the Jews who had been there were dead. He told me I was wrong: the Germans had apparently planned to slaughter them all, but fortunately, the Russians arrived before the Germans could carry out their plan.

Wife:	Rosa	
Children:	Shoshanna*	Esther*
Grand-children:	Tal	Nadav
	Dan	Sarah
	Gal	Adi

*Children of Sarah, of blessed memory

Miriam Wolberg (nee Apfelderfer)

Born 1930 in Verecke, Hungary. Refugees without Hungarian citizenship expelled across Dniester, August 1941. Massacre in Kamenitz-Podolsk, September 1941. Back to Hungary. Life in Hungary without citizenship till German arrival. Possibility of going to Eretz Yisrael rejected, January 1944. Deported to Auschwitz, spring 1944. Meets father, who works in *Sonderkommando*. Death march; stay at Rechlin and Ravensbrueck camps. Liberation; in hospital at Malchow and convent in Prague. Zionist training camp in Hungary till move to Eretz Yisrael.

'Some trace must remain!'

The transports from Hungary to Auschwitz kept coming in the summer of 1944. I was in Auschwitz-Birkenau Camp A. I had been chosen with a group of 2,000 girls from my block and other blocks to work at sorting the victims' effects at Brzezinska. They gave us blue dresses with white polka dots and white head kerchiefs, and we marched there every morning. Brzezinska wasn't far from crematorium 4. As in all the other crematoria, smoke came out of the smokestack, but here we also saw smoke rising from the ground behind the trees near the crematorium. Later I learned that there they burned in pits the bodies they weren't able to dispose of quickly enough in the overworked crematorium. One morning, not far from the crematorium, we met a group of 17 men, all of them turned quite brown, who said they tended the fires in crematorium 4. I recognized one of them as a neighbor from home and decided to try to talk to him the next day: maybe he would know what had become of Papa. The next day, before I could call out to him, I heard a cry: "Miriam!" – and that group passed us by. We didn't run into them again, and for some time I wondered whether it had all been my imagination, or whether it had really happened and Papa was alive.

In August I was assigned to the weaving workshop. We made nylon strips. I don't know exactly what for. The workshop was on the edge of Camp B-2, and every morning on our way to work we passed close to the men's camp. Among the work foremen was a decent Jew named Ackerman. I managed to make contact with him and tell him I thought Papa worked in the *Sonderkommando*. He simply replied: "Tomorrow."

When we passed by the next morning, I heard someone call to me from the roof of one of the barracks belonging to the punishment squad: "Miriam!" It was Papa.

A stone was thrown addressed to me, and one of the girls picked it up and passed it to me. That day I received Papa's first note. For three weeks I actually saw Papa during our daily morning march, and if I didn't see him Ackerman passed me a piece of bread or a note from him. All the notes said the same thing: Miriam, be strong, you must remain alive, some trace must remain! I didn't know if he meant a trace of the family or a trace of the Jewish People. In one note he wrote: "The One-on-High has a great account to settle with us; who are we to argue with him?!" I have often wondered how a Jew going through all that could still be so full of faith. I saw him in the course of two months. Two weeks before his death Papa was transferred from the camp to quarters near the crematorium. On October 7 the *Sonderkommando* revolted, crematorium 3 was blown up, and the workers were shot – Papa included.

In his last notes he wrote that he was to be sent on a transport and I was not to worry about him. And he reiterated: "I have a big thing to ask of you: You were always a strong one – you must hold out! You must remain alive! The whole family has arrived; they are at rest." I didn't understand what he meant: "You must remain alive!" I took his testament as a command to live. Till meeting him I had been apathetic. If not for our meeting I would not have had the strength to go on the death march of January 18, 1945. After all that suffering, after a severe bout of typhus, alone, with all my sick comrades left behind – if not for Papa's command I would never have been able to go on that march, wrapped in a blanket, stepping on corpses along the route. His command impelled me to go on living.

There is one thing I would like very much to do: go back to Auschwitz, to the place where Papa died, and shout: "Papa, I remained alive!"

Husband:	Dov			
Children:	Shlomo	Tzvi	Ofra	Esther
Grand-children:	Tzofit	Hodaya	Netanel	Shmarya
	Ella	Yehuda	Efrat	Yaacov
	Tal	Uri	Ya'ir	Shira
	Yael	Issachar	Rahel	Avraham
	Tzur	Tzofiya	Noa	
	Chen		Elyashiv	
			Emuna	

97

Shraga Shemer

'And I shall plant them on their soil'

> Why did the Blessed Holy One show Moses a bush burning without being consumed? Because Moses had thought that the Egyptians might destroy the Jews, so God showed him a fire burning without spending itself, and said to him: "Just as this bush is burning without being consumed, so will the Egyptians not succeed in consuming the Israelites."
>
> *Midrash Exodus Rabba 2:5*

These fragments of testimony by members of Nir Galim succinctly sum up the most terrible of the horrors that ever visited our nation. Each person with his and her particular story, each individual with his and her particular memories. The comrades whose testimonies are cited in this book are among the founders of Nir Galim, a *moshav shitufi* on the Mediterranean coast north of Ashdod, affiliated to the Iggud Hamoshavim of the Hapoel Hamizrahi Religious Labor Zionist Movement. The Nir Galim's founders are all Holocaust survivors who sooner or later made their way to Eretz Yisrael as part of the great flight of the survivors from Europe.

When World War II ended, these "witnesses" were all in their teens or early twenties, ravaged by suffering and hunger, feeble in body and wounded in spirit. On returning to their native places from which they had been deported to the labor and death camps, many of them discovered that they were the sole remnants of their families. These "brands plucked" from the great conflagration felt helpless, impotent, in this new situation, all alone in a hostile, cruel world, with no one in sight to help them.

Activists of the Bnai Akiva Religious Zionist Youth movement, also young men and women who had survived the Holocaust, realized the gravity of the situation, and also that that was a fateful moment for the future of the Jewish

98

People as a whole and the future of those survivors as individuals. Quickly they set about the sacred task of rescuing those young survivors. The activists in Europe were assisted in this rescue operation by emissaries from Eretz Yisrael. Bnai Akiva's main work was finding those children and bringing them to the training centers or children's villages that had been set up throughout Hungary. There the children were prepared for life in Eretz Yisrael, under a program that included the study of Hebrew and Jewish history, Jewish religious subjects, the history of Zionism, and the general studies that had been interrupted by the war and the deportation of the children to the ghettos and labor and death camps. At the training camps for the older youth, they learned mainly agricultural work, in preparation for kibbutz life in Eretz Yisrael. Agricultural-training centers were set up on farms that had belonged to Jews before the war and whose owners now placed them at the disposal of Bnai Akiva. Training centers were also set up in villages where non-Jews leased their lands to Bnai Akiva in exchange for a percentage of the yield. Naturally, all this cost a great deal, and the funds were provided mainly by the American Jewish Joint Distribution Committee, which worked very hard to help rehabilitate the survivors.

The grim picture described above was changed radically thanks to the energetic labors of the Bnai Akiva activists. Life at the training centers and children's villages were filled with content, and hope was infused into the youth, the great hope of reaching Eretz Yisrael and starting a new life there. This hope and the faith that it would be realized gave those young men and women the strength to trek over mountains, sneak across borders, cross rivers and seas, from the displaced-persons' camps in Europe to the "illegal immigrants'" camps in Cyprus. They took every possible path, and some impossible ones as well, to get to their destination, the Land of their great dream, the Land in which all their hopes would be fulfilled, the Land in which they would be partners in the grand enterprise of rebuilding the Jewish national homeland and where they would build homes for themselves and establish families.

The founders of Nir Galim trained at two centers in Hungary, during several periods. One center was established at Miskolc in northern Hungary soon after the war ended. It was called Miha, an acronym for *Mittel Hachshara*, Yiddish-Hebrew for "Middle Training Center," that is: for boys and girls aged 14-17, and the first group training there called itself by the Hebrew name "She'ifa," that is: "Aspiration," reflecting its members' aspiration to get to Eretz Yisrael as quickly as possible.

The She'ifa Hachshara nucleus of 20 left Hungary at the end of 1945, joined by 10 other children. Their longest stop was at a displaced-persons' camp in Germany, at Ashav, not far from Munich, where they stayed about a year. They spent the year mastering Hebrew and studying other subjects, and working in the camp's vegetable garden and in the various workshops set up by ORT (Organization for Rehabilitation through Training). At Ashav, She'ifa split into two groups: the original 20, who were older than the 10 newcomers and more experienced in working together as a group, decided to form themselves as a separate group, calling themselves "Ge'ula Hachshara," that is: "Redemption Training Nucleus." They kept this name in the "illegal immigrants'" detention camps in Cyprus, during their studies; work and the War of Liberation while at the Mikve Yisrael agricultural school; during their advanced-training period at Kibbutz Sde Eliahu; and until they reached Nir Galim as one of the settlement's founding nuclei.

The second group did its preliminary training at Cered village in northern Hungary, on a farm belonging to Dr. Shimshon Friedmann, of blessed memory, himself a Holocaust survivor. In exchange for a percentage of the yield he let these young people use his lands to train themselves for agricultural work in Eretz Yisrael.

The group, founded at the beginning of 1946, functioned till 1948 as "The Cered Hachshara" (as they continued to be called in the transit camps in Italy, during their advanced-training period at Kibbutz Be'erot Yitzhak, and until they arrived at Nir Galim as one of the founding nuclei). During this period, it was joined by members of other *hachsharot* from Hungary, and its membership ranged from 25 to 30 persons during its low period and 35-40 in its high period.

In 1948 the group sold its property and sent the proceeds to Eretz Yisrael, where they were used to buy Nir Galim's first truck. This was the group's last act before leaving Hungary.

On reaching Eretz Yisrael, the group's members were enlisted into the ranks of the Hagana, the official underground self-defense organization of the Jewish community of Eretz Yisrael, which, on the establishment of the State of Israel in May 1948, became the Israel Defense Forces. They fought in the Negev, in the Beit She'an Valley, and in the Dan Region. Several of them fell in the fighting.

The third component of the founders of Nir Galim were a group of discharged soldiers, who joined after the War of Liberation ended.

Most of them, however, did not care for the *moshav shitufi* form of life and left during the first year.

From kibbutz to moshav shitufi

Why did the Ge'ula and Cered groups, both of which had trained for kibbutz life, decide to establish a *moshav shitufi* instead – the first such settlement of the Hapoel Hamizrahi movement?

Before we answer this question, let us examine the differences between those two forms of cooperative settlement. The kibbutz and the *moshav shitufi* are based on the same ideological principles. In both, the basic production tools and resources – land, water, equipment – and all property are under the exclusive ownership of the cooperative association. This applies also to all real estate not serving the productive branches – land for housing, public buildings and the like. In the *moshav shitufi*, the settlement's governing bodies decide where the members will work. Members' incomes are paid directly into the common treasury. Budgetary allotments are not based on grade or extent of productivity, but on need according to size of family and number of children. The common treasury covers expenditures for education, culture, recreation, health and all public services, as well as health-care and old-age insurance.

So far, the kibbutz and *moshav shitufi* forms are almost identical. Where they differ significantly is in the forms of family life. In the kibbutz, all of the family's needs are provided by the kibbutz, to the extent that all members eat their meals in the common dining hall. In the *moshav shitufi*, each family eats in its own home and is allocated a budget that it is free to use as it sees fit.

Here it should be noted that an increasing number of kibbutzim have gone over to this form of budgetary allocation. It should be remembered that in the late 1940s, when the founders of Nir Galim decided to adopt this form, the principles guiding kibbutz life and the kibbutz social framework were much more rigid. Furthermore, I don't think a far-reaching socio-psychological study is needed to prove that at that time, the founders of Nir Galim, who had been bereft of their families at such an early age, felt alone in the world, suffering from the lack of a family framework. Therefore, they found the *moshav shitufi* form, which provided for a more traditional type of family life, more to their taste.

The family as the basic social unit has been a permanent feature of Nir Galim. On Prof. Moshe Davis' initiative, Nir Galim "adopted" the Bnai Amoona Congregation of St. Louis, Missouri, of which Bernard Lipnick was Rabbi, for some years. Every summer children from Bnai Amoona would spend about eight weeks at Nir Galim studying, working and engaging in recreational activities.

The first item on the study program was, naturally, the family unit.

It may be assumed that that same yearning for family has influenced other aspects of life at Nir Galim.

Another reason for adopting the *moshav shitufi* form has to do with a sad situation that obtained at the end of the 1948 War of Liberation. The two nucleus groups, Ge'ula and Cered, had trained in settlements of the religious kibbutz movement, Hakibbutz Hadati. That movement suffered heavy losses in the war. All the Etzion Bloc settlements fell to the Arabs, and many members of the Negev kibbutzim that had to be vacated left their groups. Many others were conscripted into the Israel Defense Forces and some of them did not later return to their kibbutzim. As a result, Hakibbutz Hadati decided not to establish any new kibbutzim but to strengthen the existing ones. Accordingly, the two Nir Galim groups were to remain at the kibbutzim where they had trained.

The people rejected this decision. They wished to establish something of their own – a new settlement in which they would build their own homes. In the end, they left Hakibbutz Hadati and established a settlement within the framework of Iggud Hamoshavim, enabling them to choose the *moshav shitufi* form. They were greatly helped by Michael Hazani, of blessed memory, who was then head of Hapoel Hamizrahi's Agricultural Center and saw to it that their enterprise was recognized by the movement's organs and that they were allocated suitable land for their settlement.

From Nir Vagal to Nir Galim

Discussions on the group's future went on throughout the summer of 1949, while the two nucleus groups were at Sde Eliahu and Be'erot Yitzhak. After they decided to leave Hakibbutz Hadati and set up a *moshav shitufi*, they were joined by a group of demobilized Orthodox soldiers then forming themselves into a settlement nucleus. The latter wished to establish a *moshav shitufi* that would support itself from agriculture and fishing. Accordingly, they called themselves "Nir Vagal," meaning "Fallow and Wave."

The first members of Cered and Nir Vagal arrived in July 1949 at the uncompleted building of the Kerem B'yavneh Yeshiva. The building had previously served the survivors of Kfar Darom in the Gaza District area conquered by the Egyptians, who had gone to a new settlement site in the spring. The members of Ge'ula arrived a few weeks later, after completing their training at Sde Eliahu.

In that building, which is today the main study hall/synagogue of Kerem B'yavneh, the three nucleus groups consolidated themselves into one large group and got themselves ready to move to their settlement site. Three main matters preoccupied them at that time:

1. Forming a solid group capable of establishing a self-sustaining settlement;
2. Shaping a lifestyle for a settlement that would be innovative in two respects: an Orthodox *moshav shitufi* and an Orthodox settlement living from farming and fishing;
3. Livelihood, plain and simple.

Livelihood proved to be no problem, because the members were ready to do any honest labor. They worked at loading building-sand at the plant owned jointly by the kibbutzim Yavneh and Bnei Darom (later Nir Galim joined the partnership); in citrus groves abandoned by the Arabs, which were managed by the Custodian of Abandoned Property; in vineyards of farmers of nearby Gedera and Gan Yavneh; as hired laborers at Kibbutz Yavneh; and at any other work available in the area.

In October, Nir Vagal nucleus got their first allocation of land. A group of them promptly went to the site, moved into an old Arab well-house and started fencing off the site and building bungalows.

The following spring the group got substantial reinforcement: the graduates of classes 26-27 of the Mikve Yisrael Agricultural School.

Discussions about the settlement's character as a farming-fishing village went on through the summer of 1950. I have already mentioned that the budgets of members of a *moshav shitufi* are based on the size of the family. Some of the Nir Vagal members, however, insisted that those engaging in fishing should also get part of the profits from that enterprise, because of its unusual nature – the work being harder than conventional farm work and requiring extended absences from home. At a meeting that lasted through the night, 60 per cent of the members decided that budgetary allocations would be strictly according to family size, including those engaged in fishing. The next day, most of those supporting the idea of extra budget for the fishermen left the settlement.

The fishing boat the group had bought and which had already been used for fishing was sold; the Greek instructor, George, was dismissed; and that was the end of Nir Vagal's fishing industry. Those who remained were now able to concentrate on studying the soil and climatic conditions and learning which crops to plant.

At that time the Jewish National Fund's Names Committee changed the settlement's name to "Nir Galim," meaning: "A Fallow of Waves."

The settlement's site

To a certain extent, the original group's plans dictated the choice of the site: the fishing/farming combination necessitated a location near the sea. The settlement authorities offered the group three sites. One, near Rosh Hanikra in the north, was rejected out of hand for one simple reason: Hapoel Hamizrahi's Agricultural Center has always advocated the establishment of Orthodox settlements in clusters, which greatly simplifies the provision of educational, cultural and religious services, by the establishment of regional schools and other institutions. In the Rosh Hanikra there was no other Orthodox settlement and none were likely to be established.

The second site offered in the Carmel mountain range, where the Orthodox settlement Nir Etzion is situated today. The third was the area of the abandoned Arab village of Arab-Sukreir, west of Kibbutz Yavneh, an area earmarked for a bloc of Orthodox settlements.

At that time the survivors of the Etzion Bloc, which the Jordanians had captured, were also seeking a place to re-establish themselves. They wanted to settle on the Carmel near the village of Ein Hod, an area that resembles the Etzion Bloc more than the flat Sukreir region. As a result, Nir Galim got the Arab-Sukreir lands.

That area, comprising some 10,000 dunams (2,500 acres), was abandoned by the local Arabs in March 1948 after men of Arab-Sukreir ambushed and murdered 11 Hagana members from Rishon Letzion and Ness Tziona who were patrolling the Jewish-owned citrus groves in the area. The whole village fled in fear of Jewish vengeance. In addition to Nir Galim, Bnei Darom, also an Orthodox settlement, was established on those lands. The area also contains groves and orchards planted and managed by the Yachin-Hakal company.

Nir Galim today

Veteran residents of the area remember the stories about the luscious tomatoes grown in the soil of Sukreir. It is said that after the tomato plant was placed in the soil, just one cup of water was poured into the hollow that sufficed for the entire growth period.

Such is the soil of Sukreir – today Nir Galim.

For many years the people of Nir Galim supported themselves by raising various vegetables. Much of this produce made its way to the tables of those who could afford the price in various European cities, and Nir Galim earned about 90 per cent of its income from agriculture.

The development of nearby Ashdod city and its industrial zone, containing factories that pollute the air and harm the area's vegetation, made it necessary for Nir Galim to give up much of its agriculture and seek other sources of livelihood. In recent years, it earns only about 40 per cent of its income from farming – raising cotton, sunflower seeds and fodder and operating a dairy farm, a poultry run and an apiary. The remainder comes from such enterprises as its Hof Ashdod transport company, a petrol station, a restaurant, an iron-rolling plant, and various other services.

When the younger members entered the work force, there was an increase in the number of members working outside Nir Galim, mainly women, some of them teachers in various schools in the area.

Today Nir Galim numbers some 400 persons, including 200 adults (100 families). About 40 families are of the second generation. Other children born at Nir Galim are today scattered throughout Eretz Yisrael, many of them in the villages and towns of Judea, Samaria and the Gaza District.

The Nir Galim veterans pride themselves that nearly all their children are following in their footsteps, in the path of Tora and manual labor. Nir Galim offspring have not emigrated from Israel, as have the younger generations of so many other agricultural settlements. The children of Nir Galim attend the co-educational school at Kibbutz Yavneh till grade 8-9. The boys generally go on to the Bnai Akiva yeshiva high schools and the girls to the *ulpenot*, yeshiva-type schools for girls. Many of them have gone on to university, with some then returning to Nir Galim to establish families and homes and others, as noted, going to other settlements.

For 32 years Nir Galim had its own rabbi, Rabbi Ben-Zion Firrer, of blessed memory, who died in the summer of 1988. The present rabbi is Tzvi Arnon. Nir Galim takes pride in the Synagogue on the knoll established by Isaac and Annie Keiser, of blessed memory.

The members of Nir Galim commissioned the writing of a Torah Scroll in memory of their kin who perished in the Holocaust, and the Scroll is used in their synagogue.

At the suggestion of Bnai Akiva veterans from all over Europe, Nir Galim has set up a documentation and memorial center for the Religious Zionist Movement in Europe since the movement's inception. Testimonies are being gathered, existing material is being arranged and catalogued, and research is already being conducted with the help of the movement's veterans and Bar-Ilan University students.

The serious economic crisis in all of the country's settlement movements has affected Nir Galim as well. And like the others, Nir Galim's members, including the younger generation, are grappling with the problem. Meanwhile, however, the fact remains that Nir Galim is one of the more successful of Hapoel Hamizrahi's settlements. Perhaps nothing attests to this better than the fact that virtually no one – except younger members who have gone on to help found new settlements – has left Nir Galim.

The reader of the fragments of Holocaust testimony recorded in this book will gape incredulously at the great miracle that the Almighty has brought to pass here: how these Holocaust survivors mustered the spiritual strength to rise up from the depths into which the enemies of the Jewish people hurled them, build a model settlement, establish families, bear healthy children and raise them to follow in their path, the path of Torah and labor.

This little anthology reflects the profound recognition of the Nir Galim veterans of the need to tell what they underwent to their posterity, in fulfillment of the Biblical command: "And you shall tell your children." By doing so they are also fulfilling the command: "Remember what Amalek did to you."

I cannot end before thanking from the bottom of my heart Prof. Moshe Davis and his wife, Lottie – honorary members of Nir Galim – for their help in bringing this effort to fruition. If not for Prof. Davis' devotion to this undertaking and his contribution to both the concept and the implementation, this book would never have seen the light of day.

Thanks are also due to the people of the Yad Vashem Martyrs' and Heroes' Remembrance Authority, to the members of Nir Galim who helped assemble the material, and to Meir Hovav, who edited the Hebrew edition of the book in such a devoted, professional manner.

Their reward shall be the perpetuation of the memory of our martyrs, of blessed memory.

Adina Ben-Shemesh

The Holocaust from a personal standpoint

The fragments of testimony in this book touch upon historical aspects of the Holocaust in general, and of the destruction of Hungarian Jewry in particular. But the book's main purpose is to focus on the people speaking of their own experiences during the Holocaust.

Such major events as the massacre at Kamenitz-Podolsk or the rout of the Hungarian Army in January 1943, to which reference is made in the testimonies we recorded, are not detailed in the fragments in this book. It seems to me that where historical comprehensiveness and accuracy are concerned, a fragment of a personal testimony cannot compete with a historical essay treating those events, just as a historical essay cannot compete with a personal account in portraying the immediacy of the experience.

The fragments were chosen for publication with the agreement of the witnesses, and after editing by them. One of them complained to me: "I thought you want to tell what happened in the Holocaust, yet you've chosen to publish a personal experience." To be sure, that fragment tells of an intimate experience; it is no more than a small piece of a broad panorama, presented from the particular viewpoint and personality of the observer/narrator. Yet, since this personal standpoint is not based in a vacuum but in a certain historical reality, it reflects that reality with its variety of problems. Thus, in the personal hurt of a girl whose report of the massacre at Kamenitz-Podolsk is not believed, we see the problem of the receipt of and reaction to information among Hungarian Jews. And the last exchange of letters between young people just after the German entry into the country vividly illustrates the Jews' confusion and their seesawing mood of fear and hope. This link between the personal aspect and the historical background is present in every fragment in the book.

Regarding the language of the accounts and of the dialogue quoted, we have tried to be as faithful to the original as possible without publishing solecisms. Accordingly, the styles of the testimonies vary according to the style of each participant.

Personal testimony differs from professional historiography also in style. The language of research is clear, direct, neutral; the language of personal testimony reflects a groping for the right word to express the personal emotion. This kind of effort characterizes *belles lettres* more than scholarly writing. People with sensitive ears will discern the surprisingly powerful expressiveness of some of the testimonies and parts of testimony.

The fragments in the book each represent only one page of the individual testimonies, which run between 20 and 40 pages each. The main purpose of this mosaic is to rouse the reader's curiosity. Our target readership was not the historian or even the student specializing in Holocaust studies, but a wider group, especially the survivors' children whom I met in Nir Galim. These young people's familiarity with the Holocaust reflects that of much of Israeli Jewish youth. It is based on a general acquaintance with the subject and natural curiosity, and is concerned mainly with the question of how people in general, and fellow Jews of their parents' generation in particular, coped with the Holocaust situation – a situation unlike any human society ever created.

Gathering testimony in Nir Galim

Every testimony on the Holocaust is at once a personal story and a story containing historical aspects reflecting the period. This applies also to the testimonies we gathered at Nir Galim. Yet there were several additional, unique aspects to the project.

Dr. Gavriel Bar-Shaked and Dr. Leon Volovici, my partners in gathering the testimonies, and I sensed this as soon as we arrived at Nir Galim. We sensed that the people saw this as an event of special significance: their tense anticipation showed it. Of the members who came to Nir Galim after surviving the Holocaust in Hungary, 46 – 60 per cent of the total – agreed to give testimony. For many, this is the first time they spoke up on the subject, and some – especially in recent years – did so by speaking sporadically, over a long period, of their experiences.

Most of them indicated in the course of giving their testimony that speaking at last was a very important experience for them. Many said that on their own initiative they would not have gone to Yad Vashem: they had overcome their inhibitions to speak because the project had become an organized, collective undertaking of the moshav.

So the Yad Vashem Archive's Testimony Gathering Section was not an initiator here, but a helper and encourager for a Nir Galim initiative.

A local historical archive

One of the many tasks of the Yad Vashem Archive and its Testimony Gathering Section is to broaden our knowledge and deepen our understanding of what befell the Jews in the Holocaust. People giving testimony – like the people of Nir Galim – do so with the feeling that they are contributing to this.

Yet I think that the people of Nir Galim had an additional motive in speaking up: a sense of obligation not only to the historiography of the Holocaust, but also to Nir Galim's historical sense. There is a recognition that the encounter of Nir Galim's founders with their past and their revealing it to their children and grandchildren has been vital to the moshav's future.

A major factor in the establishment of Nir Galim was the desire of the founders to begin a new page in their individual and collective histories. This group of Holocaust survivors from Hungary set out to create a new reality by establishing a new settlement in Eretz Yisrael. The intention was not merely to "drive out the past," but rather to *challenge* the past. Many of them long refrained from speaking of their past to their children. They saw the past as a possible threat to their present and their children's future. The decision of many of them to speak up no doubt expresses the turn in their individual and collective consciousnesses. Several of the younger generation were partners to this by helping to organize the project and collate the testimonies for the establishment of the archive.

Today, the Nir Galim archive contains copies of the recordings and transcriptions of all the material gathered. These are now available to all.

The concept behind the archive is that the roots of the people in Hungarian Jewish life, what they underwent in the Holocaust, their post-war training for life in Eretz Yisrael, and their settlement in the country are all part of one historical chain. The Zionist chapter in Eretz Yisrael is both a conclusion and a beginning. But it cannot be understood without examining what preceded it and what has followed.

Rivka Shulsinger-She'ar Yashuv

'I shall not die but I shall live...'

The Holocaust struck the Jews of Hungary in March 1944. Until then they had imagined that the tragedy of European Jewry would pass them by. Now this illusion was replaced by the hope that the retreat of the German army from Hungary would mean the early end of the war, at least on the Hungarian front.

Until that March the Germans could not shake Hungarian Jewry. But then, precisely the opposite of what the Jews had expected happened. Half of Hungarian Jewry – about 400,000 persons, all the Jews of the villages and towns – were deported to the death or forced-labor camps in Poland and Germany. Some of the men between 18 and 60 years of age were permitted to enlist in Hungarian Army labor units.

This cruel blow came so suddenly that there had been no time to think about escape, hiding, self-defense, etc. The panic-stricken communities, ignoring the instinct of many Jews, heeded the advice of their local official communal leadership and that of the central leadership in Budapest to cooperate with those implementing government orders and went to the ghettos. The transfer from the ghettos to the death camps came soon afterwards.

About one quarter of the 46 participants in the volume served in Hungarian labor units. When the Hungarian army retreated, those Jews were sent to German forced-labor camps. Some families were fortunate enough to be included among the "large families" whom the Germans sent toward the Austrian border and who remained together through the war. Several of the witnesses had fled to Hungary from other German-occupied parts of Europe. Most of them reached Auschwitz with their relatives – some to be exterminated, some to be assigned to forced labor.

Several features characterize the testimonies in this book:

The ages of the witnesses at the time of the events they describe range from 10 to 22.

Most of the adult males were sent to Hungarian labor camps, while the younger people, male and female alike, were sent to Auschwitz and from there to other forced-labor camps.

Nearly all the families were Orthodox, and a few of these belonged to Hassidic communities.

Most of the families were from small villages, some of them remote ones, with only a few living in the larger towns.

The testimonies were given more than 40 years after the events they describe.

110

In considering the complex subject of the will to live as expressed in these testimonies, we cannot ignore the considerable time gap between the Holocaust, when the events described occurred, and the giving of the testimony. Yet there is a positive aspect to this distance in both time and place. Indeed, here precisely lies the importance of the testimonies. When we see the force with which the witnesses resisted their fate, we also see the force that impelled them in their rehabilitation.

Moreover, the fact that they rebuilt their lives, the way they stood up to the vicissitudes they had to undergo to reach Eretz Yisrael in face of the efforts of the British Mandatory government to block them, their establishment of an Orthodox cooperative settlement – all this is unimpeachable testimony to the reliability of their recollections. It is not at all presumptuous to say that if the great time gap slightly blurred their memory, it by no means distorted their perception of the events.

Let us bear in mind that the overwhelming majority of the witnesses came from Orthodox families. As was the case with Hungarian Jewry in general, these families, too, had no conflict between their Hungarian patriotism and their faith and religious practice. But the realization that Hungary would not protect its Jewish subjects in time of trouble - a realization that was late in coming to all Hungarian Jews – came earlier to the Orthodox families. The Neolog and assimilationist Jews refused to see the handwriting on the wall even after the Jews of the countryside had already been concentrated in the city ghettos. The Orthodox perceived themselves as facing a greater danger – not "merely" the loss of their lives, but the destruction of the Jewish People and of the sacred Jewish values.

In the accounts of their daily struggle to stay alive in the camps – a struggle attended by starvation and arduous physical labor – there stands out the determination of the people to adhere to Jewish tradition, the tradition of their parental homes, despite the inhuman conditions and the constant mortal risk under which they lived.

Moreover, the more hopeless their prospects of emerging alive from that Hell seemed, the harder they strove not to submit, not to surrender that last spark of faith. Biological urge and religious faith joined to sustain the people's determination to adhere to the spiritual and cultural legacy their parents had bequeathed to them, and to live to see vengeance wreaked on the Germans.

The shock of Auschwitz – between collapse and faith

The first shock, which came immediately upon entering Auschwitz, released a torrent of doubt and fundamental questioning. The inner serenity of the believing Jew collapsed under those sub-human conditions of starvation, degradation, separation from family and the sight of the flaming crematoria.

This shock caused people to seek release in talking things out, in prayer. The result? A religious boy, seeing the horrendous sight of bodies being incinerated in an open fire, asks: "Is this the reward for loyalty to the Torah. What did the Jews do to deserve this?"

A young girl cruelly wrenched from her parents cannot understand why they met such a fate: they were religious, weren't they?! Why is she, the youngest child, still alive, and they were sent to perdition?

These are the sorts of questions that keep cropping up throughout the testimonies.

But there is the other side, too. "At that time, those who stopped believing collapsed sooner." Clinging to one's faith prevented collapse! This is repeated time and again. "People who had faith held out," says a witness who was a girl of 16 at the time. "I remember that not for a single moment did I lose my humanity...and I didn't violate any of the precepts commanding decent behavior to others."

Of course, in that difficult period there was no time to think, but she distinctly remembers that "we wanted to stay alive." Everyone wanted to stay alive: "People held on to life simply because they wanted to stay alive."

This determination is expressed in most of the testimonies: to stay alive by all means! In many people this determination stemmed from their hope and longing to see their parents again, their brothers, their sisters, and their refusal to believe that they would see them again "only in the World-to-Come." Many testify that despite the sight of the lifeless skeletons, their proximity to the ovens and the smoke pouring out of the smokestacks, they clung to the hope that their own dear ones were still alive, and they continued to search for them high and low in the camps.

Those impressed into the Hungarian labor units were similarly impelled: "Everyone wanted to stay alive in spite of the tremendous indifference to the idea of death... People were skeletons and weren't afraid of death... In the camp people knew very little about the progress of the war and they didn't bother themselves with philosophical problems...they concerned themselves with staying alive."

Some claim not to have undergone any religious second-thinking, to have clung steadfastly to their faith with never a doubt arising in their minds. Sometimes they attribute this to the quality of their religious upbringing. One witness says: "I felt that they wouldn't break me no matter how bad things got."

This was the only war they were able to fight unhampered.

For some, the stance they took to what they were undergoing was based on the national rather than the religious aspect. As one witness says: "The Nazis persecuted the Jews *as Jews* and not as *religious* Jews. So the issue wasn't to remain religious, or to remain a believing Jew, but simply to *remain a Jew!*"

For such people, the struggle for personal survival symbolized the struggle for national survival, the survival of the Jewish People and its spiritual/cultural legacy. For them, every single Jew's remaining alive meant the entire nation's survival. The author of the above statement adds that his faith not only never wavered but was even bolstered, in spite of all that he underwent. It was precisely in the concentration camp, he says, that he saw the extent to which we Jews are a chosen people: "Among the Jews there wasn't a single person who snatched his fellow's bread... People helped each other as much as they could... Jews always conducted themselves more humanely."

Hunger

Hunger was perhaps the greatest privation suffered in the camps. Whoever said that "A hungry person does not think" must himself have undergone hunger. And indeed, not a single one of the testimonies fails to mention hunger. The most common expression is, as one woman says, "Anything not to starve." And: "In order to be able to endure, you have to eat whatever you can lay your hand on."

A particularly shocking expression of this is one man's statement: "I took the bread from the slain man's hand and ate it."

Young people relate that in the camps, their parents made them eat non-kosher food to stay alive, while they, the parents themselves, did not eat such food. One witness recalls being told: "'Eat anything that will keep you alive.' My parents forced me to eat... Papa and Uncle made me eat sausage... They gave me their rations, too...commanding me to stay alive."

The starvation method was not enough for the Nazi murder machine. It is generally accepted that if the Nazis had let starvation and disease take their natural courses, all those shrivelled frames, the "Mussulmen," would have died and not a soul would have remained alive in the camps. But the planners of the "Final Solution" were not satisfied with the "drawn-out" process of starvation. They devised more "modern" methods – gassing and incineration, methods that left only the ashes of the doomed. The bodies of millions of Jews were turned into dust! This dust was buried in pits in Europe's soil.

Parents' last will: Carry on Jewish tradition!

Those who were not promptly sent to the gas chambers and crematoria of Auschwitz and Majdanek, those not crushed by the hard labor, those not felled by typhus and all the other diseases, those who did not die of starvation, thirst or frost – where did they get the strength to hold on to life with their last drop of blood and energy?

To be sure, in each personal account we see an element of luck in the narrator's survival. Still, it is clear that the determination to survive stemmed from a powerful desire to carry on the family's religious tradition and life style, even when all other hope seemed lost. What gave the people the inner strength to hold on was the stubborn clinging to every possible spark of Jewish living by saying the prayers, by somehow, if only in word, remembering the Jewish holy days, by noting events according to the Jewish calendar, by performing acts of mutual assistance, and, above all, by striving to fulfill their parents' last will: to survive and give living testimony.

She met her father in Auschwitz. She was only 14 then. She worked right next to the crematorium. She did not cry...did not shout...nothing mattered to her. But she always rememberd her parents' charge: "Don't forget where you come from." Her parents' charge was "to carry on the Jewish heritage" and be a living testimony for her own and coming generations. In notes her father sent through messengers in the camps or threw over the fence or across the ditch to her, he begged and urged her to "hold on so you can tell future generations." She lost the notes after the liberation, when she was ill with typhus. But she remembered the command to "tell it to the future generations," and in this testimony, she says, she fulfilled her parents' last wish.

This desire to carry on parents' traditions is expressed in various ways. For example: "I know Psalm 20 – 'A song for David: May God answer you on your day of trouble' – by heart, and I whisper it to myself to this day. Even in 1970,

114

during a terrorist attack on our outpost in the Golan Heights from which we 'miraculously' emerged intact, I remembered that 'Song for David.' My attachment to that Psalm is a vivid illustration of my fidelity to the tradition my father transmitted to me: 'Whenever you're in trouble, always recite the Psalms.' This served me as a living link to my family heritage, a heritage not even the horrors of the Holocaust could erase."

The significance of this testimony is not only that the witness literally believed this prayer, but rather that he also felt good about carrying on a tradition transmitted to him by his father. The parents had no illusions. They knew that their doom was sealed and that they had no chance of surviving. But fathers passed on the will to live to their sons, parents to their children. "And you shall teach it to your children," as the Torah commands. And this last will and testament was a challenge to the children, a challenge and a powerful prop in those dark months.

The desire to survive

Some people testify that their survival should not be attributed to their physical strength, but to their psychic stamina. One says he doesn't know why he was chosen to live on. But he isn't really searching for the answer. God willed it that way, and it had nothing to do with him; he has no doubt whatever that some Power beyond him decided his fate. During that period his mind had been at peace; he had only prayed for the strength to endure all the suffering, for the spiritual strength to come out of that Hell alive. With all his being he wanted to survive to reach Eretz Yisrael. He had been full of hope that God would give him the strength to endure... Those who will survive must go to Eretz Yisrael... This feeling enabled him to bear all difficulties.

He credits his survival with another theological thought: "Looking back – if after everything that happened to the Jewish People in the Holocaust the survivors were still capable of getting on the 'illegal' immigrants ships and coming to Eretz Yisrael and building a state – then there is no doubt that there is a Creator! Rehabilitating themselves from the Holocaust the way the survivors did, establishing families, raising children and establishing the state – all this could have happened as a matter of course, but only with the help of a supernatural helping Hand."

Mutual assistance

There is ample testimony to people's helping each other. One witness says: "Contrary to the general belief that people didn't help each other, help from strangers, and especially from an elder sister, enabled me to survive."

Another witness says as emphatically: "I survived because I was together with my brother, and we tried to help each other... We had an extraordinary desire to remain alive... The fact that we were together gave us the strength to hold out."

Two sisters relate that when they were evacuated from the camp because the Russians were approaching, one of them was unable to walk on and tripped and fell. Her sister wrapped her in a blanket and dragged this "bundle," thanks to which she survived.

Another woman relates how – also during the German retreat – two sisters whom she didn't know saw her fall and not get up, and between the two of them they dragged her along, thus saving her life.

The sudden separation from family, friends and neighbors most affected children in their teens, who went through the first and cruellest "selection" immediately on their arrival in Auschwitz, and then found themselves all alone in the lions' den. Here many testimonies tell of accidental meetings with relatives, or of neighbors' sticking close to each other, helping and encouraging each other. And many tell of being saved by total strangers who risked their lives doing so.

Praying – both dialogue and outburst of anger

Praying figures prominently in all the testimonies. The desire to say one's prayers daily in those circumstances expressed both an emotional and a psychological need beyond the desire to fulfill a religious obligation. Praying was both a dialogue with God and an outburst of anger at and frustration with Him. For the believing Jew, praying during those dark months was an act of communion for the individual with himself and between him and his Creator, and nobody let anyone or anything deprive him of the opportunity for this communion. Praying and religious observance in general in those circumstances were more than just a routine continuation of certain religious habits; doing so was a way of holding on to life in unbearable situations and at moments when death stared the people in the eye.

Let us try to understand the profound significance of the following testimony:

Praying today doesn't have the same significance it had then... I would repeat the prayer daily, praying for the Redemption...I implored the Master of the Universe to give me the strength to endure...to be at my side and help me to endure... Only a person in such a dire predicament and all alone in the world – only such a person can understand the role that prayer played then...spiritual strength greater than physical strength. There were stronger, more athletic people among us... They fell and didn't survive. Apparently they didn't have the spiritual strength to cope...

"Observing the religious precepts despite all the doubts gave one's life meaning..." Observing the precepts was a kind of testimony that there was still spirit inside the body – spirit, hope, strength to cope; a sign that the mind was still intact and functioning. Whoever lost these also lost control of his body. In the testimonies of the men we see the emphasis on holding on to one's own personal *Tefillin*. Those who did not manage to do so would get up long before the accustomed early rising time in the morning to rush to get a place in the line for a borrowed set of *Tefillin*. Nearly every testimony tells how "I put on *Tefillin* and observed whatever precepts I could," or "I had a close friend and we would say our prayers together" and the like. Those who survived especially difficult situations testify that they felt that Divine Providence was watching over them. As one person testifies: "I did not break; I continued to say my prayers regularly. Praying was part of my deep religious faith. In my prayers I had just one wish: to live to see the downfall of the Germans... The most important meaning of my survival would be seeing vengeance wreaked on the Germans. I vowed: There is nothing I want in life but to see their downfall: that would be the best revenge... I said: if there's a God and if I live to see their downfall... That was all I prayed for... And that is how I held on..."

The most moving parts of the testimonies are those telling of the praying and of the High Holy Day assemblies. Youth and adults engaged in a relentless struggle with their oppressors found it within themselves to sanctify themselves and gather in communion with the totality of the Jewish People, and it was precisely this sanctification that infused life and hope into them even in moments of profoundest grief and despair. Here is one heart-rending account:

That Yom Kippur Eve...with all the horrors...we worked only half a day... I don't know why. In the afternoon most of the inmates of the camp assembled, a huge throng... It is hard to describe what went on there. Heart-rending weeping. People came to implore the Blessed Holy One to help them live to get out of that

Hell. "They literally spoke to the Blessed Holy One: 'You! Do it!' The way you speak to a pal."...After the service, people felt some relief and they believed they would live to see the end of all that.

And on the "Kol Nidrei" service:

On Yom Kippur Eve the block chief handed out the food earlier, so that we would be able to begin the fast on time. "I also want to fast," he said. He asked us to forgive him, even though he often beat us unjustly. "We'll pray together, here," he said. "All the time I've been in a concentration camp I've observed Yom Kippur." In the middle of the "Kol Nidrei" service, the tyrannical *Lageraeltester* came storming in and saw the Jews praying. The block chief resignedly gave the command: "Hats off!" Then he explained to the *Lageraeltester* that this was the time when the Jews prayed to God to give them a good year, to grant them life. The *Lageraeltester* passed between the rows. We saw that he was checking to see who had dry eyes, but he didn't find anyone. Suddenly he let out a command, "Hats on!" and added: "I wish you what you wish yourselves. Happy Holiday!" and left without doing anything to us.

The festivals

The inmates of the concentration camps made every effort to get at least some little taste of the Jewish festivals. The Sabbath and festivals were ordinary days of back-breaking labor, and generally also days of special cruelty, beatings, executions and public hangings for failed attempts to escape or smuggle crumbs of food. Nevertheless, the survivors all recall some moments of festival joy. Many testimonies refer to Passover. Here is an especially moving reminiscence:

For Passover, we baked matzot in Bergen-Belsen and boiled potatoes. I don't remember who bought the potatoes and who bought the flour... All I remember is that we had a pot in which we boiled potatoes for those who would not eat *hametz*. I got there and was given potatoes, and I even threw some to my sister on the other side. I also got a small matza the size of my palm, and on Passover night, at the Seder, I broke it in two, ate one half and wrapped the other half in a rag and put it in my *Tefillin* bag. That would be the *afikoman* and I would take it home. I took it home, and the following year I burned it with the *hametz* before Passover.

An evening of true nostalgia took place at Purim:

In the evening we came home, as usual, drenched in sweat after a day of back-breaking work. Suddenly we heard cries: "*Minyan! Megillah*-reading! We're reading the *Megillah* on the second floor! It's Purim today! An old Jew is reading the *Megillah*!" I pushed my way through... It was a dream. We heard the benedictions, the reading, by heart. Everything was by heart... That Jew remembered... It was a holiday – without *graggers* [special Purim noisemakers], without children, without *Hamantaschen* [special Purim pastry]. We were all in seventh heaven... We were all elated, we sang, we saw our families, our brothers and sisters, our parents... It was Purim. And what a Purim!

You read and you ask

Reading the testimonies of the Holocaust survivors is a frustrating undertaking!

You see: crematoria and smokestacks, rag-draped skeletons, wizened frames crying out for a few crumbs of bread, long stretches of standing at "rollcall," backbreaking labor, degradation and the loss of one's human visage, escape attempts and public hangings, long death marches.

You read and you ask: Did such life, which defies the imagination, really take place? Surely it was only a nightmare! But reality hits you in the face!

And you stand there stunned, shocked, impotent, agape, and say nothing!

Only a silent prayer moves on your lips: God, why didn't you instruct us to help Your people, the People Israel? Forgive us for not comprehending their terrible plight and not hearkening to their outcry!

But You?! You also saw and heard! Their plea was a pure one...

Proudly and bravely they stood up to the forces of evil...

The millions of victims are the monument: the conquering heroes who in death bequeathed life to their brethren! The right to life!

The Holocaust survivors are the spokesmen and emissaries of the slaughtered millions!

This is the spirit that informs the documentation of the members of Moshav Nir Galim.

The very establishment of an Orthodox collective moshav by Hungarian Jewish Holocaust survivors on the soil of Eretz Yisrael is the product of a sublime struggle for survival of young persons who never submitted to what seemed to be their fated doom...

"I shall not die, but I shall live, and I shall recount God's deeds."

The children of Nir Galim